Good luck in your
Phil

What professionals are saying about...

STAY OUT OF COURT AND IN BUSINESS

"The value of *Stay Out of Court and In Business* to any enterprise that has one or more employees cannot be overstated. Clear and illustrative examples of familiar situations that result in litigation when ignored make this book a must resource for any manager. The authors well-serve the legal profession by providing a significant business support."

- George E. Bushnell, Jr.
Past-President, American Bar Association
Miller, Canfield, Paddock, & Stone, P.L.C.
Detroit, Michigan

"Steven Brandt is the most astute and well-informed advisor an entrepreneur could ask for—and this book could save you hundreds, thousands, even millions of dollars. If you are a business owner, you need this book."

- Scott DeGarmo
Editor in Chief & Publisher
Success Magazine

"*Stay Out of Court and In Business* belongs on every entrepreneurs bookshelf! In clear, simple language Steve Brandt explains the intricacies of legal issues surrounding small business. This book can save entrepreneurs thousands of dollars and countless headaches."

- Terri Lonier
small business expert and
author of Working Solo

"Too often legal matters and costs are under-managed. This book is vital for all levels of management in companies that want to grow."

- Gary L. Riley
Segment President
Allegheny Teledyne, Inc.

"This book will save you time, money, and, maybe, your company."
- James M. Osterhoff
former CFO, US West

"This book clearly and concisely summarizes the universe of law that applies to small business. A herculean task! As a lawyer and CEO, I enjoyed every word."
- Nancy R. Wendt
CEO, Squaw Valley Ski Corporation

"The contents would have saved me a lot of trouble."
- J. Frederick Merz, Jr.
CEO, Scott Specialty Gases

"Great preventive medicine. This book will help managers curb litigation."
- Robert R. Tufts
Attorney, Jackson, Tufts, Cole & Black

"This book is a must-have. Even "busy managers" will find valuable guidance. Highly recommended."
- Susan J. Scully
Human Resources/Service Industry Consultant

"A great resource. Preventative medicine. Should be required reading for anyone in business or studying business management."
- Robert K. Jaedicke
Former Dean, Stanford Graduate School of Business

"Covers legal issues in plain English. Refreshing. An important book for anyone building a business."
- Sharon Hooper
President, World Disc, Inc.

STAY OUT OF COURT
AND
IN BUSINESS

EVERY BUSINESSPERSON'S GUIDE TO MINIMIZING LEGAL TROUBLES

by

Steven C. Brandt
and
STAFFORD FREY COOPER
Attorneys
A Professional Corporation

Archipelago Publishing

Stay Out of Court and In Business
by
Steven C. Brandt
and
STAFFORD FREY COOPER

Build Your Business Guides is a registered trademark of Archipelago Publishing and the Global Management Exchange.

Book Design & Layout: Bruce Conway, Friday Harbor, WA

Published by:

Archipelago Publishing
P.O. Box 1249
Friday Harbor, WA 98250
(800) 360-6166 Fax: 360-378-7097
info@gmex.com
http://www.gmex.com

Library of Congress Catalog Card Number: 97-73783

ISBN: 1-888925-10-8

Distributed to the trade by Independent Publishers Group
(312)337-0747/ (800)888-4741

Printed in the U.S.A.

∼TABLE OF CONTENTS∽

NOTICE AND DISCLAIMER

This book is an overview of current legal concepts and issues affecting businesses. It is not legal advice. Each business has unique legal needs and situations, so the law may affect one business differently than another. Further, the law changes regularly and may vary from one jurisdiction to another. Accordingly, the authors disclaim any liability for action taken or not taken based on the material in this book. Simply stated, the specific legal issues affecting a given business require specific analysis and specific solutions. This book, by its general nature, cannot provide such analysis and solutions.

∼ *ABOUT THE AUTHORS* ∼

STAFFORD FREY COOPER is a law firm based in Seattle, Washington. The firm was established in 1905 and today it serves a diverse group of business clients made up of manufacturers, retailers, wholesalers, and individuals engaged in a broad variety of industries—from manufacturing to high technology. The members of the firm who served as the primary authors of this book have extensive experience working on matters ranging from corporate planning to commercial litigation. The attorneys below co-wrote *Stay Out of Court and In Business* to provide practical, general guidance to people who are busy building businesses.

J. William Ashbaugh	Scott D. Bissell
Michael C. Bolasina	Romney R. Brain
Meredith W. Dorrance	A. Richard Dykstra
Michaelanne Ehrenberg	Thomas M. Fitzpatrick
Larry E. McMullen	William L. Neal
David J. Onsager	Phillip L. Thom
James P. Wagner	James T. Yand

Steven C. Brandt co-wrote this book with the attorneys above. He is an experienced entrepreneur, company president, author, company director, and faculty veteran of 21 years at the Stanford University Graduate School of Business in the heart of Silicon Valley in California. At Stanford he has taught general management subjects to over 4,000 executives and MBAs. Brandt has BSME, MBA, and PhD degrees, and he has written four popular business books including *Entrepreneuring* (3rd Edition) and *Focus Your Business*. He also has a video series, *Managing the Emerging Company*.

∽ *PREFACE* ∽

This book is written to be used. It is aimed at helping people in business shrink their legal problems—to zero if possible. Just about every management person I know actually *hates* getting involved with claims, counter-claims, suits, and worst of all, court and litigation. Doing so involves time and money and, in most cases, it subtracts huge bites of brain power and energy from the on-going tasks of building the enterprise. Legal troubles frequently become uncontrollable; they assume lives of their own. Disputes or honest disagreements throw off sparks which are fanned into flames as people with different agendas are drawn into a particular conflict. The flames often escalate to a conflagration which produces a pall over the entire organization. Spark prevention is the heartbeat of this book.

Our thesis is that *the number of legal sparks is unlikely to diminish any time soon.* Legislators are working overtime at lawmaking, and court-made law, known as "common law," is generated daily across our nation in a legal system that everyone acknowledges is overloaded. Much of the activity is aimed at businesses because business, in general, dominates the center stage of our society these days.

In decades past business shared the stage with other actors and actresses. Politics was in the spotlight during the Cold War years; the military before that. Religion used to play a major role. Exploration once was the lead. Although economic self-interest has always been around, in these times, our times, it has risen to a new height in terms of popularity as an organizing principle. And the ticket to economic self-interest is money. Where is money most easily found? In the pockets of the star at center stage. Business is in spotlights coming from all directions—social, technical, economic, political. Business is where the action is.

So legal challenges and issues are not going to go away any time soon. But they can be systematically minimized by the people who make up a specific company, for their particular business. This book points the way.

The law of the land is a fact of life. It is an integral part of a system that has produced over 25 million new jobs in the last dozen years and a social order which is doing pretty well at adjusting to peace. There are a finite number of areas in which companies are most likely to get into legal difficulty. They are covered in this book. With a general knowledge of the law and a list of specific actions you can take to live within it, you can *prevent* claims from arising in the first place. And a company without legal troubles has a competitive advantage.

Steven C. Brandt
Senior Lecturer in Management Emeritus
Stanford University Graduate School of Business

～ *INTRODUCTION* ～

The grounds for making legal claims against businesses have grown like weeds in the past twenty to thirty years. For example, only a short time ago sexual harassment and employment discrimination issues were virtually nonexistent, and major product liability and intellectual property disputes were rare. Today, such subjects are governed in intricate detail under federal and state law which has spawned a whole new litigation industry. Issues that used to be quietly passed off to attorneys to handle have now become part of the day-to-day agenda for operating a company. *People in management without a working knowledge of the law of the land are at a disadvantage.*

The purpose of this book is to give operating people a general background in subjects where businesses commonly encounter legal difficulties. This book is a primer, of necessity, because law is complicated; for example, it often varies from state to state. But experience shows that the best way to minimize legal troubles is to proactively eliminate the basis for potential claims. Too often business people end up *reacting* after a claim is filed, rather than acting in advance of such a possibility. For this reason, in each chapter the authors outline action steps that will help reduce the likelihood of claims.

The book starts off with *The Last Resort: Court,* a chapter that describes what happens when all other means of settling a disagreement—including prevention—have failed. The next nine chapters deal with what to do to reduce your chances of going to court. Chapters two, three, and eight have to do with matters involving employees, namely *Employment Discrimination, Workplace Sexual Harassment,* and *Employee Handbooks.* A large portion of legal claims against businesses today come from employees—existing, past, and potential. Chapters four, five, and nine are about primary assets including *Intellectual Property & Proprietary Rights, Product Liability,* and *Risk Management.* Chapter seven is on *Contracts,* a standard business tool and the source of countless disputes. Chapter six highlights *Unfair Business & Trade Practices*—required knowledge for anyone dealing with customers or competitors. And, finally, chapter ten is about *Choosing & Using an Attorney,* a matter of importance for the management team of any company intent on growing.

The content of the book is not intended to turn readers into pseudo-lawyers. It *is* intended to provide knowledge on basic legal/business issues so people can identify potential problems early and take action to minimize claims. Today it is not enough for a company to have good products, excellent services, and a solid strategy for growth. One big court fight can put a dent, perhaps a fatal dent, in any one or all three. Today business people must also *consciously* work smart within the vast array of laws which are woven around businesses because they are the blocks in the economic foundation of our society. This vital role can be viewed as a burden or, more usefully, as an opportunity. Speaking for the authors, we see it as the latter.

Romney R. Brain
STAFFORD FREY COOPER

1

THE LAST RESORT: COURT

"It's easier to stay out than to get out."
-Mark Twain

OVERVIEW

Today there is an epidemic of litigation involving businesses of all types and sizes. In the last few years the number of court cases has soared and observers say that for every court case there are numerous cases settled outside of court. The epidemic has many supporters as well as many detractors. A large proportion of business people view legal battles with disdain, as a distraction. The fact is, however, the epidemic is unlikely to subside any time soon, and the more quickly owners and managers see legal problems as *business* challenges rather than darts from hell, the sooner they will move to control them. As one senior executive puts it: "Legal matters are about the most *under-managed* cost of being in business."

Unless they are prevented in the first place or resolved out of court, legal difficulties end up in court. Litigation is the last resort. As the Chinese proverb in chapter seven puts it: Once an issue gets into court, it takes two oxen to draw it out! Why is this so? It is important to understand that the American civil justice system is modeled on the English system imported by our colonial forefathers. It is fundamentally an adversarial system. This means the parties to a dispute (the adversaries) each present their evidence and views on the issue to a neutral fact finder—typically a judge or jury—whose responsibility it is to decide the issue based upon the evidence presented by the parties. **A lawsuit is actually nothing more than a fight to the finish** between adversaries where, in most cases, one side will prevail and the other will suffer a frustrating, and frequently costly, defeat.

Litigation might bear the trappings of a very civilized process, but in reality it is, quite simply, a verbal fight with each party's goal being victory in the dispute. Whether the issue is employment discrimination, workplace sexual harassment, product liability, copyright infringement, contract performance, or whatever, the parties in the dispute will not get to court as litigants if they do not each feel they are "in the right" in the fight. This chapter is aimed at taking the mystery out of the litigation process, minimizing the number of legal battles, and draining the emotion from those that do occur in order to make way for systematic, rational, cost-effective decisions about litigation.

A SHORT STORY

The following simple story is designed to provide a basis for this material on minimizing legal troubles connected with litigation.

Carol is the owner of a coffee stand located on a busy downtown street corner. She serves hundreds of customers on a typical weekday morning. After several years of hard use, Carol's Italian espresso machine falters. She analyzes the cost of a new machine and the potential sales from it, and she decides to proceed. It is a rational decision. She orders a new machine from Leo, a distributor of high-quality Italian espresso makers. The price is $3,000, a big sum for her. The new machine arrives a few weeks later and, over a weekend, an installer working for Leo replaces Carol's old machine with the new one. The installer runs the new machine through a brief series of tests and tells Carol it is ready to go for Monday morning. However, on Monday after an hour or so of use, the pump in the new machine fails. Carol is unable to serve many of her customers. In a panic she contacts Leo who tells her that it will be ten days before replacement parts can be obtained from Italy.

Carol continues to operate her stand during the ten-day period, but because she is unable to serve many of her customers, business drops off substantially. During the same ten days someone opens a competing coffee stand on the other side of the street. Even when the replacement parts arrive and Carol's new machine is finally operating properly, she notices that her volume of business is at least 20 percent lower than it was before the problems with the new machine arose. Carol believes that Leo and the espresso machine company he represents should be responsible for her losses.

Carol explains the situation to the lawyer who helped her incorporate her business. He tells her that even though it sounds to him

15

like she has a great case, he has not tried a lawsuit in over 15 years. He also tells her the local courts are backlogged so it might be two years before her case gets to trial. Also, he points out to Carol the language contained in the standard purchase contract Leo had her sign. It reads:

> *All products supplied by Leo's Coffee Services are warranted against defective materials or workmanship for a period of one year after purchase. We reserve the right to replace or to repair at our shop or an authorized repair facility. Purchaser's rights and remedies under this warranty are limited to the reasonable costs of repair or replacement and shall not include any claims for lost business revenues or profits or other consequential damages.*

Finally, the attorney asks Carol whether she thinks Leo, who operates his business out of his apartment, has enough assets to pay a judgment if Carol prevails in a lawsuit.

What are the issues in this short story?

There are emotions involved, of course. Carol is frustrated and disappointed. She believes in her heart that her case against Leo is simple and straightforward. There is also money involved. She had a thriving business before she did business with Leo. Now she is hurting financially. In total, all she wants is "justice," but after talking with her attorney all she sees is complications and expense. There are big questions to be answered: **Should she pursue her justice?** How long will it take and how much will it cost to do so? Why will it take so long and cost so much? Will there be a payoff? What will be the payoff? The answers to these most reasonable questions are not simple, and Carol's decision whether or not to pursue justice becomes even more difficult when it is the product of a jumble of economics and emotion.

Here are the major legal questions that would need to be answered by or for Carol:

Who would she sue?

The choices include at least Leo, the espresso machine manufacturer, and the pump manufacturer who supplies pumps for the expresso machine.

On what basis would she sue?

There are a number of possibilities: Breach of contract, breach of warranty, and product liability are the obvious ones.

What about the contract Carol signed when she purchased the machine?

Are there grounds to say that it intentionally misstated things (fraud), or was she forced to sign it by Leo? As a practical matter, did Carol even read the contract before she signed it. (If not, her case is diminished.)

Where, in which court of law, should Carol initiate her suit, state or federal court?

What remedies or damages would she seek in the suit?

How much damage can Carol actually *prove* she suffered from the out-of-service machine?

In short, the filing of a lawsuit is a serious undertaking requiring time, effort, and a series of decisions. And once it is filed, a whole sequence of events is initiated. Many of the events will involve Carol and require time and thought, if not money.

Upon receipt of a notice of being sued, Leo and/or the manufacturers—or their representatives such as attorneys, insurance companies, etc.—start turning their own wheels to prevail against Carol in the issue. **Remember, it is an adversarial contest.** They, too, will look at the signed contract, the product delivered, and how Carol used the equipment (in strict compliance with the instructions in the manual provided?). At some point they will most likely start probing into Carol's claims of damages. In the legal process of discovery (see details later in this chapter) they may wish to review Carol's books, interview her employees, and so on. They may even interview her new competitor! All in all, the suit will not be a trivial undertaking for either party.

Is it worth it for either party to go court? This is the big question. And the best answer is one that is a product of a vigorous **cost-benefit analysis** leading to a *business* decision, not a moral one. It is the message of this chapter that Carol is best served by deciding whether or not to sue in the same way she looked at whether or not to buy the new expresso machine: Carol needs to look carefully at the costs involved...and the potential returns.

More on Carol later in this chapter.

THE LITIGATION PROCESS

The first step in filing a lawsuit is often to consult an attorney. It is possible for people to represent themselves in some situations such as in small claims courts, but in cases of any complexity, attorneys are almost a necessity for the reasons shown below.

What law applies?

Someone, an attorney or not, looking at a possible suit must first review the law applicable to the dispute. Relevant law flows from three sources. There are **statutes**—laws enacted by state legislatures, the U.S. Congress, and, in some cases, city and county councils. There are **administrative regulations**—rules (with the effect of law) issued by bodies such as the federal Environmental Protection Agency, Food and Drug Administration, and the Securities and Exchange Commission. And finally, there is **common law**—the body of law that flows from prior court cases. Common law includes cases from England which date back several hundred years, but most common law used today is from cases in the past 25-30 years.

Which court has jurisdiction?

All states and the federal government have court systems in which lawsuits are decided. *Most cases are handled in state courts.* If a business has a dispute with individuals or companies outside its own state, or if the dispute involves a matter of federal law, e.g., employment discrimination or copyright infringement, the dispute will probably be handled in a federal court. There are federal courts in or near most major cities. State courts are typically located in each county seat.

There are also courts of limited jurisdiction that typically handle minor matters. Small Claims Court is such a court. These courts, which exist in every state, handle smaller cases and have relatively relaxed procedural rules.

How is a suit initiated?

A person files a "Complaint" with the court clerk in the chosen court. It is a brief, written statement about the nature of the claim and the amount being claimed in damages. There is normally a filing fee of $50-250. The clerk of the court then arranges for a "Summons" to be served on the person or company being sued. In the story, if Carol files a complaint, Leo, at least, will be served with a summons. The summons would advise Leo that a lawsuit has been filed against him and ask him to respond with a written "Answer," usually within 20-60 days.

In the answer, a "defendant" (or defendants) either admits or denies the charges made by those filing the suit (the "plaintiffs"). In many cases the defendant will also make claims back against the plaintiff by filing a "Counterclaim" with the answer. A defendant may also file a "Third-Party Complaint" if he or she believes another party should be involved in the case. All third parties will then be given summonses they must answer, including counterclaims, third-party complaints, etc.

What happens after everyone is on notice of a suit?

After the complaints and answers are filed, the parties embark on a legal process known as "discovery." Here, all the parties exchange relevant documents, ask questions in writing (called "interrogatories") of one another, and question key witnesses and parties, under oath, in what are called "depositions." This step in a suit can be *very* expensive depending on the complexity of the case. Sometimes it can take years to complete!

When is there a jury?

Trial is usually scheduled after discovery is completed. In most state and federal courts today, it typically takes at least 18-24 months after the initial filing to get to trial. Usually the parties involved determine whether the case will be decided by a jury or by the judge. Normally a jury will be used if any party involved requests a jury trial. There are different opinions about when and if a jury trial is preferable over a "bench" trial in which the judge decides on the merits of the case.

Occasionally cases are resolved by a judge without a trial if either the plaintiff's claim or the defendant's defense is determined to be without either factual or legal merit. In such cases, the judge grants a "Motion for Summary Judgment" which resolves the case. Such motions are rare.

What are appeals?

A party who is unsuccessful in a trial may appeal the outcome to the appropriate Court of Appeal, state or federal. The basis of an appeal must be that a *mistake* was made in the original trial, e.g., that the judge gave improper instructions to the jury or erred in an interpretation of the law. Appeals courts do *not* re-hear the evidence presented in a given trial; they do not deal with issues of *fact*, only issues of *law*. Reversals of trial courts by appeals courts are also rare.

In summary, all of these litigation process steps are potentially present in the simple espresso machine story. When a businessperson like Carol or Leo gets involved with litigation, regardless of the amount in dispute or the size of the companies, she or he faces a series of decisions. The decisions that have to be made are best made as *business* decisions, not *legal* decisions, per se. *They should be made primarily on the basis of the costs and the potential benefits of proceeding.* Legal matters may dictate the alternatives, but the decisions should be business decisions just like capital expenditures, product pricing, and whether or not to respond to a competitive threat of some kind. Too often, because courts and attorneys and opponents are involved, pride or ego or anger gets woven into the fabric of the decisions. Such decisions have an impact on people and ultimately the business, whatever it is. A cool head is an asset when it comes to litigation.

HOW TO MINIMIZE
YOUR LEGAL TROUBLES

Litigation is literally the last resort. Ideally, you will take steps such as those outlined in the chapters that follow to avoid lawsuits. However, most companies do end up in court at some time or another. Here are steps designed to make the experience as positive as possible.

 1. Decide whether or not you need professional help, and, if so, what kind.

Except in very insignificant matters, you will probably be well-served to at least consult with an attorney qualified to give you an opinion on the litigation matter at hand. As you will see in subsequent chapters, the law is vast, complicated and changing continuously. People spend professional lifetimes keeping track of current conditions. You need to deal objectively with the reality of the times in order to minimize your legal troubles.

 2. Select professional help to fit your particular needs.

Quite often an attorney who assists you in corporate or tax matters is not experienced in in either litigation or in a substantive area such as employee relations, product defects, or personal injury, that is central to your case. Make certain that you are represented by an attorney who is comfortable with the litigation process and who thoroughly understands the area of law involved as it can be extremely complicated.

First and foremost, pick and work with an attorney who is familiar and comfortable with litigation. Attorneys knowledgeable about setting up corporations, raising money, negotiating contracts, or dealing with state or federal agencies may be weak at handling litigation effectively and efficiently. Many attorneys who specialize in business transactions rarely, if ever, go to court. If you are the manager of a baseball team which desperately needs a good pitcher, you would not hire a shortstop to fill that role, even if he or she is the best shortstop in all of baseball. Even though pitchers and short-stops are both baseball players, they have different roles and need different skills if they are to excel in their positions. The world of attorneys is like a big baseball team: different attorneys excel at different areas of legal practice. When you are faced with a litigation issue, you need to seek assistance from a professional who is experienced in handling litigation in the area of law in which you are involved.

 3. Get a realistic evaluation of the merits of your case.

It is important that you ask your chosen attorney for an honest assessment of the merits of your case, pros and cons. Unfortunately, some attorneys give their clients overly optimistic evaluations, particularly early in the process. At the same time, some clients only want to hear good things about their cases; they filter out anything negative. However, an unrealistically sunny analysis sets up false expectations and often leads to disappointment and disillusionment when things do not work out as projected. **When you are faced with litigation, you do not need a cheerleader.** You need a strict teacher who will tell you the facts of legal life and where you most likely stand on the (adversarial) issue at hand.

So, once again, ask for and obtain a realistic assessment of the strengths and weaknesses of your case as early in the sequence of events as possible. With the passage of time, positions tend to harden. Obviously, an attorney hearing about your case for the first time will be reluctant to give a definitive assessment of your prospects on the spot. He or she will need time to review the facts and applicable law. Then, an attorney's evaluation of the case may change over time as important facts regarding the case come to light. It is important to note, too, that an attorney's evaluation of a case is no guarantee of any particular result. Most every case decided in court has a loser and a winner even thought both sides thought they had a winning argument going in! An attorney's evaluation of the merits of your case is one piece of information you need to make informed business decisions to minimize your legal troubles and expenses.

In particularly complex cases or cases involving large potential damages, it is often useful to obtain a **second opinion** on the merits of your case. Select another attorney qualified to give you an informed decision just as you would select a second physician to give you a professional opinion on a vital health matter.

Finally, you should consider, and ask for input on, the pros and cons of alternative methods of dispute resolution such as arbitration or mediation. Because of the time and expense associated with court proceedings, many businesses today are turning to mediation or binding arbitration to speed the resolution of disputes. Mediation and arbitration are similar in that they each involve resolution of disputes outside the courtroom. They are, however, different from one another in some important ways.

Mediation is, typically, a *non-binding* process whereby the parties involved work with a neutral mediator in an effort to come to a mutually-acceptable settlement of the dispute. In other words, a mediator is an individual who works with the parties in order to come up with a compromise settlement which all sides can accept.

In contrast, **arbitration** is usually a *binding* process whereby a neutral arbitrator makes a final decision in the case, just as a judge or jury would do if the case proceeded to trial. The advantage of arbitration is that it can frequently lead to a resolution much more quickly than going to court, and often at less cost. In addition, arbitration may be advantageous in cases involving highly complex or technical issues. In such cases, an arbitrator with considerable background or experience in the particular industry or trade may be able to make a much more informed decision on the dispute than can a judge or jury lacking in such background.

Needless to say, courts burdened with an ever-increasing case load encourage parties to utilize mediation or arbitration whenever possible. However, it is important to understand that **arbitration and mediation are both voluntary processes** which must be agreed to by all parties. Along this line, it is quite common these days for agreements between businesses to state that any disputes will be resolved by arbitration. This is done to save time and money, and to reduce the stress that often accompanies litigation headed for, or in, court.

 4. Obtain a realistic estimate of the cost and time that will be required.

A clear picture of what is required to see a case through trial is critical to making informed business decisions with respect to litigation. Such an estimate should be requested early in the process, and competent litigation attorneys should be willing to provide an estimate without undue delay. Your attorney should be able to estimate the number of hours she or he or others will have to spend preparing for and trying the case. You should also know the hourly rates to be charged.

She or he should also be able to estimate the approximate date it is likely the case could go to trial as well as when such important, pre-trial activities such as depositions, can be expected to take place. You should also ask your attorney to estimate the amount of time which you and other people in your company will have to devote to the litigation process prior to and during trial. **One of the great, hidden costs of litigation to a company is the value of the time you and others *must* devote to a lawsuit.**

5. Do a cost/benefit analysis of each new situation as it unfolds.

Throughout the life cycle of a litigation issue, business decision-makers should be constantly evaluating the evolving costs and potential benefits of the case. Obviously, such an analysis should be made prior to starting a lawsuit if you are the plaintiff, or commencing to defend against a claim if you are the defendant. Just as important, however, business people should continue to evaluate the situation as the case proceeds and more is learned about the relative strengths and weaknesses of the case. Quite often, things can change dramatically as fresh facts are uncovered, new issues are raised, or uncertainties are resolved. Throughout a case, you should assess: Is what we are doing worth the time and expense? In short, you should keep your cost/benefit analysis updated. If the ratio exceeds the number one, it is time to examine your alternatives.

6. Stay Involved.

While it is usually important to have professional input, you or your management team should make the major decisions such as whether or not and how to proceed from any given point. One of the most common mistakes business people make, particularly those who are new to litigation, is they **rely too much on their attorneys.** Disputes are business matters; a given case is your case, not your attorney's. His or her job is to help you and your company in the lawsuit, not to make the key decisions. You need to stay involved... and objective.

Litigation often triggers strong emotional reactions. It is not unusual for the parties, whether plaintiff or defendant, to feel abused, cheated, harassed, and/or persecuted. While these feelings are understandable, rational *business* decisions are still what is needed as a case develops. Decisions made in the heat of the moment or with half-information are usually not the optimum decisions for the business involved.

Most owners and managers find dealing with litigation to be both unpleasant and unproductive. While this may be true, it does not change the reality that litigation occurs, just as do tax audits and government safety and/or health inspections. These "annoyances" are among the costs of doing business in these times.

CONCLUSION

So what should Carol do? In the short story of the Italian expresso machine early in this chapter there is probably not much Carol could have done to prevent her predicament. She purchased what she deemed to be a high-quality piece of equipment she needed from someone who appeared to know what they were doing. Unfortunately for Carol, the equipment had a defective pump which the manufacturer replaced. Carol's sales declined while she was waiting for the new pump. Now she is at a fork in the road. Should she proceed with a lawsuit against the distributor, Leo, and the other potential defendants? Doing so involves an investment (time and money) in litigation with an uncertain outcome in terms of her financial well-being.

She has an alternative. Carol can also invest her limited time and money in promoting her business. For example, she could spruce up her coffee stand, do some advertising, perhaps add a new stand on another corner nearby, expand her product line, or even explore buying out her new competitor. These investments, too, have an uncertain outcome in terms of her financial well-being in the future.

Carol has a decision to make, and it is not necessarily an easy decision. But it is a *business* decision.

2

WORKPLACE SEXUAL HARASSMENT

"Is the law on our side?"
–Shakespeare, Romeo and Juliet

OVERVIEW

Sexual harassment litigation has exploded in recent years. The explosion is due primarily to the passage of the Civil Rights Act of 1991 and an increased and increasing public awareness of sexual harassment in the workplace. The 1991 Civil Rights Act allows people who claim they are victims of sexual harassment (plaintiffs) to request jury trials. The Act also allows the plaintiffs to seek both compensatory and punitive damages from the defendants which in most cases are companies. Publicity, jury trials, and the widening array of damages being handed down in the courts in recent years may be encouraging employees with sexual harassment claims to pursue them by initiating litigation. In earlier times such employees

29

might have chosen to remain silent or to pursue less litigious avenues of relief or satisfaction.

Many employers are responding to the challenge. In general, such employers adopt anti-harassment policies and provide training designed to eliminate sexual harassment incidents in the workplace. In spite of such policies and training, the litigation boom continues to grow. **Recent state and federal court decisions make clear that it is insufficient for employers simply to draft anti-harassment policies and investigate internal complaints.** Rather, to protect their companies from liability, employers must aggressively enforce stringent anti-harassment policies and take prompt remedial actions for transgressions. Even after instituting an anti-harassment policy, employers must **demonstrate an executive and managerial attitude of zero tolerance** for violations as a show of their commitment to the company policy. The actions outlined below are means of instituting and supporting anti-sexual harassment policies.

THE LAW OF THE LAND

Title VII of the Civil Rights Act of 1964 says that it is *an unlawful employment practice for an employer . . . to discriminate against an individual with respect to compensation, terms, conditions, or privileges of employment because of such individual's...sex.* Sexual harassment is classified today as one form of discrimination, and the definition of what actually constitutes sexual harassment continues to evolve in our legal system. As litigation on the matter increases in volume across the country, courts are identifying behaviors that fall within the legal definition of sexual harassment. The courts are also identifying behaviors that are not considered sexual harassment, i.e., behaviors that withstand scrutiny under a reasonableness standard. As an increasing number of types of workplace behavior are found to fall within the sexual harassment boundary, employers are generally well served by being aggressive in an attempt to both prevent and correct sexual harassment incidents. The more vigorous the programs, the better the chances of avoiding liability.

SEXUAL HARASSMENT CLAIMS

There are four major issues that may lead to claims:

General Harassment

Traditionally, Title VII litigation required that sexual harassment claims rest upon sex and sexual conduct. Recent judicial decisions, however, have enlarged the range of incidents which can be used as the basis for a harassment claim. For example, an allegation of gender-based animosity will now sustain a sexual harassment claim. This means that harassing, abusive, and crude remarks may constitute sexual harassment even though a manager or supervisor directs the comments to all of his or her employees, both male and female. **Where a manager's or supervisor's conduct is so severe and pervasive that it alters the conditions of employment and creates a hostile, abusive work environment, a court may sustain the claims of a sexual harassment plaintiff.** In addition, the law recognizes that male employees may suffer sexual harassment at the hands of female co-workers or managers. Male plaintiffs have successfully sued their employers for sexual harassment by their female supervisors.

Same-Sex Harassment

With respect to same-sex harassment, the courts differ about whether Title VII prohibits same-sex harassment. One federal court held that a male supervisor's harassment of a subordinate male employee was not actionable, despite its sexual overtones. The court reasoned that Title VII seeks to eradicate an atmosphere of oppression by a dominant gender, not by the same gender. Other federal courts, however, hold that Title VII is not limited to heterosexual harassment and that same-sex harassment is actionable under Title VII. Individuals may regard sexual advances as unwelcome regardless of the offender's gender. Further, state courts have permitted plaintiffs to pursue same-sex harassment under state law. The issue of whether same-sex harassment is actionable under Title VII is one that will likely be resolved in the near future. The U.S. Supreme Court recently accepted a case on this issue for review.

Harassment based upon sexual orientation, however, is not actionable under Title VII. Courts reason that Title VII prohibits harassment on the basis of gender, not sexuality. Harassment of homosexuals and lesbians is potentially offensive toward men and women in equal measures. Therefore, harassment of lesbians and homosexuals because of their sexual orientation does not qualify as gender discrimination actionable under Title VII.

Quid Pro Quo Harassment

The law recognizes two forms of sexual harassment for which an employer may be liable. The first is quid pro quo (one thing in return for another) harassment. This type of harassment occurs when either (1) unwelcome sexual favors are a condition of one's employment; or (2) unwelcome sexual favors are sought by threatening or actually causing a tangible detriment to one's job. Employees generally assert quid pro quo claims against managers or supervisors when they find themselves forced to choose between submitting to a manager's or supervisors' personal demands and the loss of job benefits, promotions, or employment. Most courts that have dealt with quid pro quo sexual harassment claims **have held the employers involved to be strictly liable on public policy grounds**. In general, when management people are found to have abused their authority, employers are declared liable because they were the parties best suited to prevent such abuse.

Until recent years, courts required quid pro quo harassment plaintiffs to demonstrate that they suffered tangible economic detriment as a result of their manager's or supervisors' unwelcome sexual advances. Recent court decisions, however, indicate an erosion of the "economic harm" element. One federal court held that a quid pro quo plaintiff need only show a "threat" of economic harm, rather than actual economic harm. Another court found that a supervisor's threat to make life difficult for the plaintiff if she did not resume a relationship with him constituted a detriment to the plaintiff's terms or conditions of employment. Because the supervisor linked non-hostile working conditions to acceptance of his sexual advances, he was harassing her in a quid pro quo manner even though she did not suffer actual economic loss. The disintegration of the economic harm element has reduced the burden of proof on the plaintiffs in quid pro quo harassment suits.

CASE A: Patricia was employed as a waitress at A's Bar & Grill. A's was owned and operated by B Enterprises and managed by Donald. While working at A's, Patricia was subjected to continuous sexual harassment. The harassment consisted of unwelcome sexual comments and physical contact from Donald. At one point Donald offered Patricia two hundred dollars of his own money to have sex with him. Some time after she refused, Patricia noticed that her hours of work were decreased. Another time Donald suggested to Patricia that she could become an assistant manager at the Bar & Grill. The offer, however, was linked to Patricia's acquiescence to Donald's personal proposals. Patricia refused again; she did not receive the promotion. Soon thereafter she did not receive an anticipated salary increase. Donald indicated that she did not receive the raise because she refused to have sex with him. Patricia filed suit against A's Bar & Grill and B Enterprises. The court held that B Enterprises was strictly liable for the quid pro quo harassment perpetrated by Donald and awarded monetary damages to Patricia.

In Case A the court held the corporation strictly liable for the sexual harassment by its manager, Donald. The decision was justified because the manager relied upon the actual or apparent authority inherent in his supervisory position within the company to extort sexual favors. Because the employer vested actual or apparent authority in the manager, the employer was held to be strictly liable for the misuse of that authority.

Hostile Work Environment Harassment

The second form of harassment for which employers may be liable has to do with the general work environment. To establish a sexual harassment claim in this area an employee must demonstrate three things: (1) That a supervisor or co-worker made sexual advances, requested sexual favors, or engaged in physical conduct of a sexual nature. (2) That the conduct was unwelcome. (3) That the conduct was sufficiently severe or pervasive to alter the conditions of the victim's employment and create an abusive working environment. In addition, in assessing whether a workplace environment qualifies as hostile, courts usually look at factors such as the frequency of the discriminatory conduct, the severity of the discrimination, whether the offender physically threatened the complainant or uttered offensive statements, and whether the conduct un-reasonably interfered with an employee's work performance. Incidents that are relatively trivial or isolated will typically not lead to a finding of employer liability for a hostile work environment.

> *CASE B: A male employee at a manufacturing plant frequently used sexually explicitly language around a female co-worker and frequently touched and fondled the female co-worker. The female employee lodged complaints with the plant supervisor. The supervisor took no action for several months and the harassing conduct continued. Finally, the male worker was transferred to a different shift. Other male employees, however, continued his course of intimidation. The woman finally resigned from her position and filed suit against the employer.*

In this case the court found that the female had established the requisite elements of hostile work environment harassment and awarded monetary damages. The harassment was unwelcome; the employee was singled out and suffered the harassment as a result of her gender, and the harassment was sufficiently severe and pervasive to alter the conditions of employment and create an abusive working environment. The court held the employer responsible because the employer knew about the harassment but failed to take reasonably prompt and adequate corrective action.

While most hostile work environment lawsuits are aimed at unwelcome conduct that occurs within the confines of the workplace, some lawsuits have to do with conduct between employees **outside the workplace.** For example, recent cases have included incidents which occurred at out-of-town business conventions and at after-hours social gatherings. An employer's liability for situations involving off-premises conduct is not automatic. The law remains unsettled as to when and if a hostile work environment can include events outside the normal work place. While intuitively it might seem that off-premise conduct lies outside the realm of employer responsibility, off-premise work may be inextricably entwined with job-related responsibilities. To guard against liability for any such harassment, employers should make sure their written policies cover off-premises work. Then, employers should treat complaints involving off-premise incidents with the same seriousness given to other complaints of sexual harassment.

To summarize on hostile work environment claims, when an owner, manager, partner, or corporate officer is found to have personally participated in harassment, courts automatically impute the harassment to the employer. On the other hand, when an employee's co-worker perpetrates the harassment, an employer will be liable only if the complainant demonstrates that the employer (1) authorized, knew, or should have known of the harassment and (2) failed to take reasonably prompt and adequate corrective measures. Courts hold that employers had actual or constructive knowledge of the harassment if the complainant either registered a complaint at the managerial level or the harassment was so pervasive that the employer should have known about it. An employer will be liable for such harassment if it fails to take remedial action reasonably calculated to end the harassment.

HOW TO MINIMIZE
YOUR LEGAL TROUBLES

The intent of the law as it is being interpreted in the courts over time is to reduce to zero the incidents of sexual harassment people encounter in the course of their employment. To comply with the law, employers need to proactively seek to eliminate sexual harassment within their organizations. Following are six actions business leaders can take to stay in compliance with both the spirit and letter of the law of the land.

1. **Set expectations. Write and maintain a written anti-sexual harassment policy.**

The creation of a written anti-sexual harassment policy is a big step toward setting the stage for desired behavior. The written policy should explicitly define and prohibit sexual harassment, explain the procedures for filing a complaint with an independent representative of the employer, and encourage the prompt reporting of all complaints. The policy should contain assurances that all complaints will receive thorough, impartial investigation and resolution; that investigations will remain confidential to the extent consistent with an employer's obligation to investigate; and that all personnel, including executives, managers and supervisors, are equally subject to the policy.

2. **Broadcast expectations. Let every employee know what is expected.**

An anti-sexual harassment policy loses its effectiveness quickly if the only copy of the policy is buried in the personnel manager's desk! Employers need to ensure the wide dissemination of the policy—first to existing members of the organization, and then to new people coming aboard. Experience shows that compliance with policy provisions and the effective utilization of incident reporting procedures depend upon employees' familiarity with the policy. Copies of the policy should be included in employee handbooks (see Chapter 8); copies can also be posted on employee bulletin boards. Some progressive firms include mention of the policy in their in-house newletters.

 3. Establish crisp reporting procedures.

An effective reporting system will enable employees to present their complaints and concerns to their employer quickly and without fear of retaliation. **Trust is an essential factor in implementing an effective reporting procedure.** Employees will not report claims if they believe they will face ridicule, inaction, or retaliation. Fostering trust requires leadership that includes an open, sympathetic ear for employees with harassment claims. More specifically, experience across a cross-section of companies indicates that it is best to identify more than one individual to whom employees can report complaints. In addition, it seems to be productive if there are several channels for complaints such as in person, after hours, via suggestion box or interoffice mail, or at staff meetings. For cases in which the designated individual or an immediate supervisor is the offender, the company needs to institute a procedure for bypassing those individuals. Some companies appoint an outside individual, such as a director or the firm's outside legal counsel, to serve as an alternative vehicle for registering harassment concerns. An employer should treat verbal and written complaints with equal seriousness.

4. Investigate complaints promptly.

Upon receiving a complaint, a designated and properly-qualified individual should promptly investigate the situation. The investigator should guard against conducting the investigation as an inquisition. Rather, the investigation should proceed as a fair and impartial fact-finding process that leads to an objective decision. The employer should consider using two interviewers during the investigation: one to interview the complainant, alleged offender, and any other necessary witnesses, and one to note the facts as they emerge during the interviews. The interviewers should not presume the guilt or innocence of either party until they have concluded the investigation. Throughout any investigation all parties and witnesses should feel confident that they will not face retaliation for participating. The interviewers (and employer) should seek a fair and impartial investigation and resolution. What is done should appear fair and impartial to outside observers. Employees who receive fair treatment are less likely to later file a lawsuit.

If the investigation is inconclusive, the investigators might wish to inform the accused employee that appropriate disciplinary action will follow the discovery of additional information. The accused employee should be aware that retaliation against the complainant will result in disciplinary action. The employer or investigator should periodically check with the complainant to ensure that the harassing conduct has ceased and that the employee does not perceive that he or she has been the victim of retaliation.

Prior to issuing a disciplinary decision, the employer should provide the accused employee an opportunity to be heard and to present rebuttal evidence. By providing all the parties with minimum "due process" safeguards, employees are more likely to feel that they have been treated fairly. If the investigation reveals that offensive conduct did occur, the employer should take prompt remedial action designed to stop future harassment. The discipline of the offender should match the severity of the conduct. Depending upon the nature of the harassment, the remedial measures could range from a verbal warning to counseling, suspension, transfer, demotion, or termination.

5. Conduct anti-sexual harassment training.

Anti-sexual harassment training is an essential supplement to a written policy. A written policy alone may prove ineffective in defining harassment. A portion of the people in almost any business organization usually require concrete examples of appropriate and inappropriate conduct. Proper training provides an opportunity to demonstrate and discuss the propriety, or impropriety, of specific workplace behavior. For example, some employees might be unaware that certain conduct, such as sexually-explicit language, touching, and off-color jokes, is offensive to particular co-workers. Discussions, which can be a part of the training sessions, allow employees to voice their discomfort with particular behavior. Training sessions give the trainer a chance to explain the law and encourage employees' cooperation and understanding. For example, new or untrained employees might be unaware that their conduct violates the law and the company's policy. One other important benefit of training is that employees' questions may expose potential problems. Then an employer can take corrective action before little problems grow into big ones.

A final word on training: Periodic repeat sessions reacquaint employees and managers with the issue of workplace sexual harassment. By keeping the issue out in the open, employees are less likely to engage in prohibited conduct and employers are less likely to face lawsuits and liability. Such training sessions also reaffirm an employer's commitment to the anti-harassment policy and to the employees' welfare in general.

6. Stay current.

The definition of, and liabilities for, sexual harassment conduct is evolving over time as complaints, claims, and lawsuits wind their way through our judicial system. People involved in building businesses are wise to take steps to remain abreast of developments in both state and federal courts.

CONCLUSION

Reducing the risk of lawsuits and liability is just good business. Employers need to be vigilant in their attempts to eliminate sexual harassment incidents across their organizations. Leadership backed up by written policies and training are the best tools for achieving this end. Sexual harassment, or claims thereof, are embarrassing to everyone involved, and they are disruptive. Morale, productivity, and self-esteem are all affected.

A growing body of federal case law confirms that employers may avoid liability for the acts of individuals by taking action to eliminate harassment. In addition to publicizing and disseminating a strongly-worded, anti-sexual harassment policy, employers need to institute effective reporting and resolution procedures. Then they must act resolutely on complaints. Employers may successfully insulate themselves from liability by promptly investigating claims and responding with remedial measures designed to deter future incidents of sexual harassment.

Stay Out of Court and In Business

3

EMPLOYMENT DISCRIMINATION

"I can try a lawsuit as well as other men, but the most important thing is to prevent lawsuits."
–Confucius, Analects, Bk. xii,. (c. 500 B.C.)

OVERVIEW

It is virtually impossible for an employer to ever actually "win" an employment discrimination lawsuit when all the costs involved are considered. Such suits are disruptive to the ongoing life of a business, expensive to defend, and an unpleasant experience for everyone involved—from employees to supervisors to owners and executives. The only practical way to win is to conduct your business in a way that makes claims obviously frivolous in the first place.

Many people in management do not acquire a working knowledge of the law governing employment discrimination until a charge is filed with the EEOC (Equal Employment Opportunity Commission) or their company (and sometimes they themselves) is sued.

The horse is out of the corral at this point. The key to minimizing legal troubles with discrimination is a pervasive knowledge of the law, a steady, even compliance across an organization over time, and thorough documentation. This can be accomplished by knowing the law, following the law, and committing your personnel-related activities to paper to create an evidence trail of your knowledge of, and adherence to, the law. There are two other chapters in this book that relate to employment issues, namely, Chapter 2 on Workplace Sexual Harassment and Chapter 8 on Employee Handbooks.

THE LAW OF THE LAND

The law pertaining to employment discrimination is complex. It differs from one federal circuit (geographic area) to another, from state to state, and from city to city. Therefore, there are potentially at least three overlapping laws (federal, state, and city) that may apply to any given employer in a particular circumstance. This chapter will provide you with a general overview of the law with a special emphasis on federal law because it applies to most businesses across the country and is the law on which most state and local laws are modeled.

At-Will Employment

The general rule in the United States is that employees who do not have written employment contracts are considered "at-will" employees. With at-will employees, an employer can terminate, demote, promote, or change the terms and conditions of the employment, with or without notice, and with or without cause. **The laws**

prohibiting employment discrimination constitute a major exception to the doctrine of at-will employment. Under laws enacted by Congress and virtually every state in the United States, *it is unlawful for an employer to take adverse action against an applicant or employee that is motivated by the applicant's or employee's status as a member of a protected class.* Examples of adverse action can include termination of a longtime employee, refusal to hire an applicant, and less favorable treatment of an employee with regard to pay, bonuses, promotions, or other terms and conditions of employment.

Protected Classes

What are the protected classes? They are identified by federal statutes, state statutes, and local ordinances. Under Title VII of the Civil Rights Act of 1964, it is an unlawful *employment practice for an employer...to discriminate against an individual with respect to compensation, terms, conditions, or privileges of employment because of such individual's race, color, religion, national origin, or sex.* Under the Age Discrimination in Employment Act of 1967, most individuals who are at least 40 years of age are designated as a protected class. The Americans with Disabilities Act of 1990 protects individuals with disabilities (including HIV+ status, and people recovering from alcohol or drug addiction) who *can perform the essential functions of the employment position that such individual holds or desires...with or without reasonable accommodation.* Other federal acts protect people who have had difficulties with debts or who are in the armed forces. Some state statutes and local ordinances include sexual orientation and marital status as protected classes. The laws against employment discrimination do not protect only minorities. For example, Caucasians receive the same protection from Title VII as racial minorities, and, absent a legitimate affirmative action program, they may sue if race was a motivating factor in an employment decision. In summary, business people should be careful that they do not make employment decisions based on a person's...

Race
Color
Pregnancy
Religion
National Origin
Sex
Age
Disability (in certain instances)
Membership in the armed forces
Past history with debts or bankruptcy

Jurisdictional Limits

Most federal anti-discrimination laws do not apply to small employers. Under Title VII and in the Americans with Disabilities Act, an employer must have **at least fifteen employees** for the statutes to apply. Under the Age Discrimination in Employment Act, the employer must have **twenty employees**. State and local versions of the federal anti-discrimination laws have their own jurisdictional limits. For example, the threshold in the State of Washington is eight employees; in Seattle the number is four.

Damages

Prior to legislative amendments in 1991, the remedies that a successful, aggrieved party (plaintiff) could obtain for a proven violation of Title VII were equitable in nature. For example, the plaintiff might receive back pay, reinstatement to a lost position, front pay if reinstatement was not available or appropriate, and the payment of reasonable attorney's fees and costs. In addition, the Age Discrimination in Employment Act provides for liquidated damages if the employer's violation was found by a jury to be "willful." (Liquidated damages are quasi-punative; they are usually calculated by doubling actual damages.) It was, and is, also possible for a court to impose other types of injunctive relief such as requiring a company to instruct all managers or employees in non-discriminatory employment practices.

In 1991, Congress amended the anti-discrimination statutes to authorize a broader range of remedies. Today successful plaintiffs are entitled to all the remedies identified above, plus the full range of compensatory damages previously available in personal injury litigation. This means that courts may require employers to pay for lost future earning capacity, emotional distress and suffering, inconvenience, mental anguish, and loss of enjoyment of life. Plaintiffs may also request punitive damages when the conduct of the defendant is sufficiently egregious to warrant them. Unlike compensatory damages, which are intended to compensate the plaintiff for any emotional or financial loss, the purpose of punitive damages is to punish the defendant and to make the defendant serve as an example for others. Under the federal employment discrimination laws, the total of compensatory and punitive damages are limited as follows:

Number of Employees	Damage Limit (Per Plaintiff)
15-100	$50,000
100-200	$100,000
200-500	$200,000
500+	$300,000

State and local versions of Title VII vary widely from the federal law. For example, in the State of Washington punitive damages are not allowed, but there is no limit on compensatory damages.

Individual Liability

It is common for plaintiffs to name owners, managers, and supervisors as separate defendants in employment discrimination cases. Most, but not all, federal courts that have addressed the issue have ruled that only the corporation/employing entity is subject to suit for employment discrimination. The state counterparts of the federal legislation may authorize individual liability, depending on the language of the statute and the interpretation of that language by the state courts. Needless to say, the stress of a lawsuit is compounded when managers and supervisors have to worry about their individual assets being at risk.

In summary on the law of the land, and repeating the point made at the start of this chapter, it is difficult to ever really win a suit involving employment discrimination. There are a variety of costs even when an employer is found not to have discriminated. It is far better to prevent claims and suits.

EMPLOYMENT DISCRIMINATION CLAIMS

There are four major issues pertaining to claims:

Disparate Treatment
Disparate Impact
Reasonable Accomodation
Retaliation

Disparate Treatment

The most common claim made against businesses is for dissimilar (disparate) *treatment*. An employee or potential employee claims that an employer treated her or him unfavorably or less favorably because of her or his membership in a protected class. For example, a male employee might allege that his employer promoted others over him because of dislike for his religion. Disparate treatment claims can be made by individuals, groups of people, or via a class action in which one person or a small group presumes to speak for a larger group as a whole.

In a disparate treatment case, the ultimate question is whether the claimant's membership in a protected class was a factor in the adverse employment decision. Under federal law, the question that would be put to the jury is whether or not the person's membership in a protected class was a "determining factor" in the adverse decision. Some states use a lower standard than the federal law. Such states say an employer is liable if the person's membership in a protected class was a "substantial factor," rather than a determining factor. In these kinds of cases, an employer defends itself by demonstrating a legitimate, non-discriminatory reason for the adverse decision, e.g., why the person was fired, or not hired, or demoted, or not promoted. **Solid documentation regarding substandard performance or qualifications** is the best way to demonstrate non-discriminatory reasons for adverse decisions involving an employee.

Disparate Impact

In a disparate *impact* case, a person challenges a presumably neutral policy or requirement by alleging that the effect of the policy or requirement has an adverse impact on a protected class and that **the policy or requirement is unnecessary for effective performance** of the job.

For example, the employment requirement of a minimum height for police officers was challenged in 1980 in one federal court case to the effect that the policy (at least 5'-8") enforced by the City of Pontiac, Michigan excluded a disproportionate number of women because they tend to be shorter than men. Further, the challenge included material to show that the height requirement was and is not necessary for effective performance of the job. Although the height policy or requirement appeared neutral on its face, the requirement was deemed unlawful by the courts because its effect was discriminatory against a protected class.

As a practical matter, disparate impact claims are quite rare in recent years.

Reasonable Accommodation

Employers have a legal obligation to show some flexibility with regard to a person's religious beliefs or practices or her or his disabilities. If an employee or potential employee can perform the "essential functions" of a job with "reasonable accommodation," then it is unlawful to discriminate against the person because of these factors. Determining what is an essential function and what constitutes reasonable accommodation are job-specific inquiries. An accommodation is not reasonable if it involves undue hardship such as significant difficulty or expense. A court in Oklahoma held that a diabetic truck driver *could* be accommdated in a situation where there were no passengers or hazardous materials involved, and food was always within reach. On the other hand, a court in Alabama found that a police department did *not* need to accommodate an officer who could not effect a stance necessary to complete a state-mandated, handgun training program because he had restricted use of his right arm and hand.

50

Retaliation

Federal law and most state laws prohibit an employer from retaliating against an employee who complains about discriminatory employment practices or cooperates in the investigation of a charge or lawsuit. Forms of retaliation include termination, demotion, suspension, isolation, etc. Also, it is important to note that a person can still seek (and win) recovery for retaliation even if it is found that the person's original complaint (that precipitated the retaliation) was without merit.

In summary on claims, disparate treatment is the most common claim made against businesses. However, although a particular claim may be made on the basis of employment discrimination, aggrieved, at-will employees also regularly include other issues such as breach of oral contract, breach of promise, wrongful discharge, violation of public policy, and intentional or negligent infliction of emotional distress. These subjects are usually governed by state law.

THE EEOC (EQUAL EMPLOYMENT OPPORTUNITY COMMISSION)

In order to pursue a claim based upon most federal anti-discrimination statutes, the initiating party must first file a formal charge with the EEOC. The deadline for filing a charge is 180 days after the last occurrence of alleged discrimination.

The deadline date is relatively easy to calculate in the case of a job termination or the non-issuance of a job offer; it is more difficult to calculate when it involves a continuing violation of some kind. Once a charge is filed, the EEOC may or may not investigate. Sometimes it will; other times it will wait 180 days and issue a right-to-sue letter to the initiating party if the party requests it. That party cannot file a lawsuit alleging a violation of a federal anti-discrimination law until after it has filed a timely charge with the EEOC and received a notice of her or his right to sue. If the person suing goes to court without having received such a notice, there are grounds for a dismissal of the claim by the court.

If the EEOC decides to investigate, the intensity and timing of its investigation will vary dramatically depending on the assigned investigator's workload and the publicity appeal of the claim. **It is difficult to predict what the EEOC will do.** An employer will be given the opportunity to respond in writing to a specific charge and provide documentation in support of its position on the matter at hand. The EEOC may then contact witnesses and subpoena documents.

Should an employer use an attorney or a human resource professional during the time a charge is pending before the EEOC? It depends. An employer needs someone knowledgeable about employment discrimination law to draft a response to the charge and otherwise cooperate with the EEOC's investigation if there is one. The key is to work with the EEOC in such a way as to avoid prejudice in any subsequent litigation or otherwise limit the range of solutions you have to the charges.

Individual states may have their own agencies which have their own requirements. Such agencies, if they exist, will often work in conjunction with the EEOC to process and investigate claims.

HOW TO MINIMIZE YOUR LEGAL TROUBLES

The intent of the law is to make people who employ other people base their decisions about employees and potential employees on performance considerations, not membership in a class of people. Separating on-the-job performance, potential or actual, from other human factors (e.g. effort, interest, appearance, compatibility, etc.) is not an easy task in many, if not most, business situations. Informed, vigilant managers are required, as is documentation of performance and decisions.

 1. Stick to job-related inquiries when evaluating applicants.

Make sure both your application forms and interviewers avoid asking questions or inviting answers that have the effect of identifying applicants who are members of a protected class. For example, a question that leads to the disclosure of the club(s) to which an applicant belongs can lead to a later claim. The general test should be: **Is the information requested necessary to judge an applicant's competence or job qualifications?**

Here are the basic guidelines about what can and cannot be pursued during an interview or on a job application:

- Do not seek information on an applicant's marital or family status, including family planning decisions, child care arrangements, or people to contact in event of an emergency. You can ask if the applicant was ever known by another name (so you can do reference checks), or whether the applicant has a relative who is employed by the company (if you have an anti-nepotism policy). You can ask how long the applicant plans to stay on the job and about his or her attendance record in past jobs.

53

• Do not pursue information regarding religion, religious holidays or practices, national origin, parents' national origin, appearance, foreign language proficiency (unless it is necessary for the position), any disability, or any handicap. A spirited debate on religion might be very stimulating, but it is definitely forbidden territory in an employment interview setting.

• You can describe the requirements of a subject job (days, hours, duties) and inquire generally whether the applicant can perform the job "with or without reasonable accommodation." The EEOC recommends that the issue of accommodation not be addressed until after you have decided to offer the applicant a position. At that point the EEOC suggests that you make an offer conditional on the candidate's ability to perform the essential functions of the job.

In essence, to minimize legal troubles connected with hiring, you are well advised to stick to an applicant's ability to perform the duties of the job in question.

 2. Establish and use a probationary period for all new employees.
While the laws against employment discrimination protect employees during a probationary period, such a period provides an opportunity for managers to systematically evaluate actual performance in the workplace. Appropriate action can then be taken early in the employment relationship with employees who do not meet the standards for the position. Moreover, an employee who is terminated during a probationary period is less likely to file a claim

than one who has been employed for an extended time. When you have a probationary period, it is important that *all* new employees be subject to it and that a record be kept of each person's progress and evaluations while on probation.

 3. **Maintain and use a comprehensive employee handbook.**

Experience indicates that both employees *and juries* respond positively to the presence of manuals that spell out key processes affecting employees. For example, when managers and supervisors follow a system of progressive discipline that is in writing for everyone to see, it is more likely an employee can correct minor problems before they boil over into major ones and termination. A proper employee handbook should set forth expectations regarding job performance and provide for recourse when those expectations are not met. A handbook should also set forth a procedure by which complaints of discrimination can be investigated and handled internally in a fair and impartial manner. **Because some states will enforce as written the terms of an employee handbook, the particular language used should be chosen with great care.** Employee handbooks are discussed in detail in Chapter 8.

 4. **Conduct and document regular performance reviews.**

To minimize your legal troubles, your company should have a formal process of employee evaluation. It should *require* supervisors, managers, and executives to honestly and objectively appraise each of their people in terms of job-related strengths and weaknesses. The process should also help evaluators identify ways in which individuals can improve their performance. This is simply good business, and many organizations do conduct periodic assessments. Where many companies fall down, however, is in documentation, particularly documentation about poor performers.

The importance of putting performance problems down on paper can not be over-emphasized.

For example, suppose a company must lay off employees in a reduction of staff. When this happens, the door is opened to mass litigation against the company because those selected for layoff will often believe (or, at least, claim) they have been singled out for reasons unrelated to their performance, e.g., age. If you have documentation that shows that the people who were selected for layoff were the less accomplished performers in the company, you will have a positive case to present to the EEOC (and perhaps, later, to a jury), or it will allow you to avoid litigation altogether. You will have evidence that your employment decisions were based on performance and merit, rather than on membership in a protected class.

Here is another example. Suppose you terminate a member of a protected class and he or she seeks help from an attorney. It has been known to happen. The first thing most plaintiff attorneys will do is ask to see their potential clients' personnel files. They will often do this before agreeing to take a discrimination case. If there is no file for the employee in question, the attorney knows the odds of winning the case are improved. Juries tend to believe that problems warranting termination should be a matter of record. If there is a file and it contains only positive performance evaluations, the attorney will know that you may well have a difficult time persuading either the EEOC or a jury that the terminated employee deserved to be terminated based on lack of performance. On the other hand, if there is a file and it identifies weak performance and/or other work-related problems over time, the attorney may well decline to take the case.

Start documenting a performance problem as soon as it arises.

5. Use severance agreements selectively.

Sometimes it becomes necessary to terminate an employee who is a member of a protected class and who is a borderline or gray-area case in terms of adequate performance. You recognize that the employee has the potential to make a troublesome claim. The person may even have threatened, either expressly or implicitly, to file suit. In this case, you should consider negotiating a severance agreement with the employee that will offer him or her "consideration" (see Chapter 7 on Contracts) in exchange for a release agreement. In a typical severance agreement, the employee agrees not to pursue any claims of discrimination against you. While you may blanch at the thought of paying severance to a borderline performer, you may wish to at least look at the economics. The cost of defending a claim in this circumstance may well be much greater than the cost of obtaining a severance agreement and release at the time of the termination.

In this regard, employees over the age of 40 have special rights when it comes to severance agreements. Under the Age Discrimination in Employment Act, any release agreement must include an express reference to the Act, a 21-day period in which to review the agreement before signing it, and a 7-day period to revoke the agreement after signing it.

6. Consider insurance to cover your employment practices.

Some insurance companies now sell policies that cover the costs involved in claims and lawsuits alleging employment discrimination. This type of insurance is relatively new, and, if available, it is a way for you to pass off some of your risk of being in business to a third party, the insurer. Since insurance companies deal with many claims from a variety of sources, they should have broader experience with employment claims than any specific operating company. Their potential participation with you may justify the cost of the premium involved. In some cases you may have or be able to obtain employment practices coverage under your Comprehensive General Liability, Errors and Omissions, Umbrella, or Homeowner's policies. As suggested in Chapter 9 on Risk Management, it is important to know what your existing policies do and do not do for you.

 7. Check your employee headcount.

Whenever an employment discrimination claim is filed or threatened, you should determine whether you have the minimum number of employees required in the statutes that are alleged to have been violated. The earlier this issue is checked, the quicker the claim may be shown to be invalid.

CONCLUSION

There is no ironclad way to ensure that your company—and perhaps, you—will not be sued for employment discrimination. However, there are steps you can take to reduce the chances it will happen. Under the law of our land, employers retain the discretion to hire or fire at-will employees for any reason or no reason at all provided there is no discrimination involved in the decision. The EEOC and juries do not accept that employers will use that discretion capriciously, however. Policies and practices such as those outlined above will help you prevent or defuse employment discrimination and claims thereof by employees—past, present, and potential.

4

INTELLECTUAL PROPERTY
&
PROPRIETARY RIGHTS

"Property has it's duties as well as it's rights."
–Benjamin Disraeli (1804-81)

OVERVIEW

Businesses compete with one another in the marketplace. They battle for customers, distribution, people, capital, favorable treatment, and advantage in general. Assets often make a difference in which enterprises prevail. More assets are usually better than fewer, and they need to be actively managed and protected as they are accumulated in the life of a company.

Assets exist in two forms, tangible and intangible. Tangible assets are things you can put your hands on such as inventory, accounts receivable, money in the bank, furniture, fixtures, buildings, and equipment. Intangible assets, on the other hand, are more illusory. They include information like customer and vendor lists, production processes or know-how, technical drawings, and business plans for the future. Intangible assets also include a business's intellectual property. A company or product name, unique logos or layouts, formulas, software designs—these are examples of **intellectual property**. Companies own their intangible assets, including information and intellectual properties, in the same way they own their buildings and inventory. Such ownership is called having **proprietary rights**, i.e., ownership rights. People in business often fail to do an adequate job of protecting the proprietary rights they have in their intangible assets, in part because they may not know what needs to be protected, and in part because they may not know the means at hand. Protecting such rights is good business and the subject of this chapter.

What does it take to protect rights and to avoid infringing on the rights of others? It takes knowledge about **what is protectable** and **how to do it**. And vigilance. In general, it is far more cost effective to take preventive measures than it is to end up in court either as an initiator of a lawsuit (plaintiff) or a defendant. But it is important to keep in mind that the primary reason to protect intangible assets, including information and intellectual properties, is that they are often the key to a competitive advantage. Tangible assets can often be purchased and are typically easily duplicable. Intangible assets, on the other hand, exist as a consequence of many hours of trial and error, are not obvious to competitors, and are difficult to reproduce independently. As with other aspects of business life, litigation about proprietary rights has increased exponentially. The actions outlined below can help business builders prevail as the importance of intangible assets continues to increase in the years ahead.

Fortune magazine writer Thomas Stewart was quoted on this subject. He gives the example of two companies, Microsoft and IBM. In 1996, he figured, every $100 invested in IBM bought $23 of fixed

(tangible) assets. By contrast, the same $100 invested in Microsoft bought about $1 in hard assets. Clearly, investors are valuing something at Microsoft that is not captured by conventional accounting techniques. That something is a somewhat amorphous asset, intellectual capital.
—*International Herald Tribune, Cashing in On Trends in Advance, Steven Pearlstein, 12/30/96. ©1996, The Washington Post. Reprinted with permission.*

THE LAW OF THE LAND

Our courts and legislatures across the country have historically sought to balance several competing interests when enacting and enforcing laws having to do with intangible assets, including information and intellectual properties. The competing interests are three in number. Owners, such as companies, seek to protect their investments in developing information, ideas, and competitive advantage. Former employees or competing business owners have a right to make a living and capitalize on their skills. And our society in general has an interest in competitive markets and the promotion of innovation. Because of these three, on-going, competing interests, our laws as written provide only a starting place. To balance competing interests, *courts tend to review each dispute on a case-by-case basis.*

The laws that exist tend to fall into one of five categories:

Trade Secrets & Confidential Information
Trademarks and Trade Names
Copyrights
Patents
Corporate Goodwill

In general, trade secret laws encourage the development of products and processes by protecting commercially valuable information which owners wish to protect from disclosure. Trademark laws focus on connecting a product with its producer so that consumer confusion is avoided. Copyright and patent laws are aimed at promoting writings and inventions through delivering exclusive rights for a certain period of time to the owners, while providing disclosure of the works to the public. Laws relating to goodwill, which may be the most intangible of the intangible assets, generally protect a company against unfair or deceptive trade practices of a competitor. Internally, goodwill as well as other intellectual or intangible rights are often protected through the implementation of company policies and agreements with employees. See Chapter 8.

PROPRIETARY RIGHTS

As indicated earlier, there are five basic categories that fall under proprietary rights.

Trade Secrets & Confidential Information

Laws in this area offer far-reaching intangible property protection to developers of ideas and information. For owners to gain trade secret protection from the courts, the material must be secret, valuable, and, in some jurisdictions, new or novel. While the "valuable" and "novel" elements may face little court scrutiny, an understanding of the secrecy requirement is crucial. Nearly 75 percent of our states have adopted some form of the federal Uniform Trade Secrets Act. It defines a trade secret as information that derives independent economic value from being secret, i.e., it is not generally known or readily ascertainable by proper means. **The act requires owners to take reasonable precautions to keep their secrets secret.** Some examples of protected trade secrets include customer and vendor lists, information on a manufacturer's production methods, formulas, technical drawings and mathematical algorithms, and in some cases, records of computer programmers' trial-and-error efforts during software development, and even portions of software source code.

Overall, the secrecy requirement has two attributes. First, the information or process must not be publicly known or ascertainable, and the owner must work at keeping it a secret. Whether or not a given subject is secret can depend upon what is "generally" known or "readily" ascertainable by "proper" means. For example, while one cannot properly seek protection of a vendor list lifted directly from the Yellow Pages, a list *derived* from the Yellow Pages is protectable after the owner has spent time and money selecting certain vendors who provide the most valuable pricing and service.

The second attribute is that **owners must treat their secrets appropriately.** Most often trade secret disputes arise because an owner has taken insufficient precautions to protect his or her material. For example, court protection can be precluded if an owner allows public disclosure through displays, trade journal articles, advertising, random use by current or former employees, unguarded transfer on the Internet, or other carelessness. Once again, vigilance is required.

Trademark and Trade Name Protection

A trademark refers to a specific good or service and is linked to the source or quality of that product or service. A trade name, however, identifies a business entity and its goodwill. Thus a trademark is a word, phrase, symbol or design, or combination thereof which identifies a company's goods and distinguishes them from goods produced or sold by others.

"Service marks" are basically a kind of trademark. They identify a specific service provided by a business and distinguish the named service from the services of other providers. Trademarks or service marks may include the use of numbers, logos, symbols, sounds, and nonfunctional product shapes. Some examples of well-known trademarks are those used by Snapple® for teas; Campbell's® for soups; Pepsi® for soft drinks; L'eggs® Panty Hose (egg-shape packaging) for hose; and COCA-COLA® (logo plus shape of bottle) for cola drinks. On the other hand, Merrill Lynch and The Boeing Company are illustrative of trade names.

Trademarks are protected by registration under the federal Lanham Act as well as through registration in the states and countries in which the mark will be used. Registration at the state level without federal registration, however, provides only marginal protection. Prior to statutory protection, trademarks were safeguarded under common (court-made) law, which still applies today. Whether by statute or common law, trademark protection can best be summarized as "use it or lose it." Such protection is limited in time and geographic scope to the period and area in which the goods are distributed or the services are provided, as well as the natural area of expansion of the business. Federal registration does, however, give you a nationwide right of priority.

If a trademark owner simply relies upon common law protection, he or she is neglecting the presumptions and remedies afforded by statute. The owner risks losing the mark in the "natural area of expansion" to someone else using the same mark who has already expanded there. Additionally, the owner must prove ownership of the mark or name, must prove the ownership is prior to that of the infringer, and that the infringement caused confusion in the mind of the consumer to the damage of the owner. Last, the owner must prove the amount of damages suffered by virtue of the infringement.

Under both statute and common law, a greater degree of protection is available for a "strong" trademark. Strong trademarks are unique and can be arbitrary with no logical connection between the mark and the goods or services—like Apple® for computers. Strong marks can also be suggestive, conjuring up an image or impression. A strong mark is rarely descriptive of the product and is not generally a surname or geographic name.

Trade *name* protection is also limited under common law to the time period and geographic area of its use, together with the business's natural area of expansion. Contrary to statutory trademark protection, registration of a trade name under federal or state statutes accomplishes little more than the protection obtained under common law.

What about the **Internet**? Recent cases suggest that the use of domain names will be analyzed according to traditional principles of trademark and trade name law. There is more on this later in this chapter in the section on how to minimize legal troubles.

Copyright Protection

As stated by the U.S. Supreme Court, the federal Copyright Act is *intended to motivate the creative activity of authors and inventors by the provision of a special reward, and to allow the public access to the products of their genius after the limited period of exclusive control has expired.* For at least as long as an author's lifetime, copyright law protects the author's profits arising from his or her original expression of a creative idea through some sort of fixed medium such as an article, book, or video or audio tape. It also protects sculptures and three-dimensional works.

The first element of a copyrightable work is **originality**. The work must be independently generated by the author with at least a minimal degree of creativity. Utilitarian articles such as bookkeeping forms, mechanical devices, and typeface designs are not copyrightable. Unlike patent law, however, originality does not mean the copyrighted work must be novel or unique. Thus, for example, the telephone company's organization of names, telephone numbers and addresses, while not novel, is copyrightable in part as a result of the creativity required to organize the information in a certain fashion.

Second, contrary to trade secret protection, a copyright cannot protect ideas; it can protect only **an *expression* of those ideas** that is "fixed" in a tangible medium. As defined by the Copyright Act, *"a work is 'fixed' in a tangible medium of expression when its embodiment in a copy or phonorecord, by or under authority of the author, is sufficiently permanent or stable to permit it to be perceived, reproduced, or otherwise communicated for a period of more than transitory duration."* For example, while transitory events such as a speech or an image on a computer screen are not tangible or copyrightable, a speech recorded on an audio tape or a computer program carrying the image for a computer screen *are* copyrightable. **If an idea, process, concept, method of operation, or discovery cannot be reduced to a fixed tangible medium, it cannot be copyrighted.** Copyright law protects only actual fixed expression and not the underlying content (idea) behind that expression.

An example of an uncopyrightable idea or method of operation is Microsoft's use of a window-like interface similar to Apple Computer's operating system. In *Apple Computer v. Microsoft Corp.*, the Court of Appeals held Microsoft's Windows program did not infringe upon the appearance of Apple's operating system since there was virtually no other practical means of designing a user-friendly, mouse-operated system. The system approached the fundamentals of a method of operation rather than an expression of an idea.

Finally, to be copyrightable, the item must consist of a **work of authorship**. Works of authorship include literary works (including computer programs), musical works, dramatic works, choreographic works, pictorial, graphic and sculptural works, audiovisual works including movies and multimedia productions, sound recordings, and architectural works.

A copyright lasts the life of the author plus fifty years. If the work was authored by someone on a work-for-hire basis, the copyright lasts 75 years from publication or 100 years from creation, whichever occurs first. Generally an author owns a copyright. When more than one person participated in the authorship, each has an undivided interest in the copyrighted product. When the author creates the product under the employ of another and within the scope of her or his employment, the employer automatically holds the copyright even though the employee was the author. This is called the **work-for-hire** doctrine.

Absent actually employing a person, another way a business can retain a copyright is to have an independent contractor/author sign a contract assigning ownership to the business of all interests associated with the work done by the contractor/author.

A copyright owner owns a bundle of rights rather than just one. For example, a copyright owner may grant the right to reproduce and distribute a computer program or book in Canada to one party, in Great Britain to another party, and in Scandinavia to yet a third party. He or she could retain the rights to distribute the material in the United States, as well as to develop, produce and distribute any derivatives of the material anywhere. In short, all rights not granted by the copyright owner are retained by that owner.

As in trademark protection, an author has common law copyright protection without the need to register. A copyright arises automatically at the moment of fixation, whether or not the work is published and whether or not it is registered with the United States Copyright Office. As soon as words are typed onto a page or music is recorded onto tape, the material is copyrighted.

However, just as with trademark protection, an owner enjoys substantial advantages if she or he **registers the copyright in a timely manner**. To protect against infringement the author is wise to register the copyright as soon as a work is published. With some exceptions, infringements which occur before a work is registered are not protected by the federal Act.

Copyrights are registered only with the United States Copyright Office; individual states have no registration capabilities. Normally, an author must submit one copy of the finished product, a completed application, the computer program (for computer software) and an application fee. If the material includes trade secrets, the author can block out certain portions of what is submitted.

Once registration is complete, the author need do nothing more to protect the copyright. Contrary to trademark protection, copyrighted material is not required to contain a copyright notice (as was the case prior to March 1, 1989). Nonetheless, a copyright notice reading © **All rights reserved**, including the name of the claimant and year of publication, should be prominently affixed to the work to provide protection in some foreign countries, to deter infringement, and to defeat an infringer's claim that the infringement was innocent.

Patent Protection

Under federal patent law, any person who *"invents or discovers any new and useful process, machine, manufacture, or composition of matter, or any new and useful improvements thereof, may obtain a patent.*" A patent gives you the right to exclude others from making, using, or selling your invention.

There are three types of patents: utility, design, and (organic) plant patents.

Utility patents cover articles of manufacture, machines, compositions of matter, and industrial processes. Examples of this type of patent include an engine, machine-crafted products such as hand held tools, mechanical devices with moving parts, a genetically engineered biological product, and a chemical treatment process.

Design patents apply to new, original and ornamental designs of manufactured articles. The shape of a boat or car could be the subject of a design patent.

Plant patents are granted to new plant varieties that are asexually reproducible. Examples of plant patents include those for fruit-bearing trees and ornamental plants like roses.

To be patentable, an invention must be new and useful. It can not be identical to something that already exists. It can not be patented if it is known or used by others in the United States, or if it is patented or described in a printed publication here or in a foreign country within a year of the date the patent application is filed. The application must be filed within one year of the date the invention is first sold, offered for sale, published or committed to public use (not including experimental use), or the patent is barred. This one-year grace period is not provided by most foreign countries.

Only one patent will be granted for any single invention. However, a single patent can be granted to several inventors. Disputes over who is entitled to a patent (in the case of simultaneous filings) is determined after a hearing by the federal Patent and Trademark Office.

Prior to 1995 a utility patent generally lasted 17 years from the date of issuance. In 1995 utility patents were increased to 20 years. Patents in effect at the time were given the benefit of the extended term. Utility patents generally require periodic maintenance fees after issuance. Plant patents generally last 17 years and require no maintenance fees. Design patents generally last 14 years and have no maintenance fees.

Goodwill Protection

After a period of advertising and operating, many companies develop a niche in consumers' minds; people recognize the company and what it represents. People feel "goodwill" toward the enterprise. It costs money to develop such goodwill. It is a business investment just like a new facility, and goodwill has value to the companies that developed it. Goodwill, therefore, is property, an intangible asset, worthy of protection.

The most common trespasser upon such property is the former employee who has left to start his or her own competing business elsewhere or a former business owner who has sold his or her business to new owners. Often such former employees or owners attempt to take some goodwill with them. The most common form of protection against this risk is a signed contract. Laws governing non-competition agreements, non-disclosure agreements, and employee invention agreements vary greatly from state to state.

Non-competition agreements are generally intended to prevent a former employee or owner from either beginning a competing business or working for a competitor within a specific geographic area and within a specific period of time. New owners should normally have sellers sign non-competition agreements as a condition precedent to a purchase. In addition, employees should be required to execute non-competition agreements either at the outset of employment or at such time as they receive an increase in job responsibilities and more salary. Although non-competition agreements are clearly a restraint of trade, most states will enforce such agreements if they are reasonable and supported by adequate consideration (see Chapter 7 on Contracts).

HOW TO MINIMIZE
YOUR LEGAL TROUBLES

Proprietary (ownership) rights are of increasing interest as our society moves toward the formation of more and more intellectual capital. The world of business is becoming increasingly dependent upon knowledge and less dependent on, for example, manual labor. There are specific steps that builders of businesses can take to protect their intangible assets, including intellectual properties. There are also steps for preventing infringements on the assets of others.

TRADE SECRETS AND CONFIDENTIAL
INFORMATION

 1. Identify trade secrets and confidential information vital to your business.

Everything you do does not fall into this category. Decide what you need to protect as part of your competitive advantage.

2. Establish policies, procedures and guidelines for protecting your property.

Employees should be provided with designated, vital information only on a *need-to-know* basis, and all employees should be subject to a company non-disclosure policy and/or a signed, non-disclosure agreement.

3. Mark all confidential documents, computer files, or other forms of information with appropriate non-disclosure warnings.

In some cases it may be necessary to post signs indicating security areas and to maintain locks, guards, alarms or closed circuit television or other appropriate measures to ensure security.

4. Have key employees, vendors, customers, shareholders or selling shareholders (of a closely held corporation), board members, potential buyers, or other parties in contact with confidential information sign a non-disclosure agreement.

The agreement can be independent of or a part of some larger agreement such as an employment agreement. The key ingredient of a non-disclosure agreement is its definition of the confidential information. Define it broadly. While the courts generally inflict fewer restrictions on non-disclosure agreements than non-competition agreements, enforcement varies from state to state.

5. Require all new employees and independent contractors to sign an agreement warranting that his or her position with your company will not violate any confidentiality requirements of any prior organization or business, and agreeing that he or she will not use or disclose confidential information from an outside work place while associated with your company.

One of the most common ways to become embroiled in misappropriation litigation is by hiring an employee or independent contractor who violates the trade secrets or confidential information of his or her prior employer or other clients (in the case of an independent contractor).

TRADEMARKS AND TRADE NAMES

 6. Complete searches prior to adopting a particular mark or name.

Seek to avoid infringing on the rights of existing users. Use a search firm or a qualified attorney to search for prior, conflicting uses.

 7. Register trademarks federally if you anticipate that your product or service will be used in more than one state.

Doing this will provide your company with protection that extends beyond what can be achieved via common law or state registration. Companies can register a mark under the Lanham Act if the mark is or may be used in more than one state. Companies may file a registration based upon actual use, or contrary to common law protection, based upon the owner's bona fide intent to use the mark. Once registered, businesses must include a notice (such as ®) with the mark to ensure application of all remedies and benefits available through federal registration. **Trade names are not registerable with any federal office.**

A certificate of registration from the United States Patent and Trademark Office is initial evidence of a valid registration, the owner's ownership of the registered mark, and the owner's exclusive right to use the mark nationwide in connection with the class of goods or services with which the mark is associated. All other providers of that class of goods or services are deemed to know (whether they actually know or not) about the owner's protected, exclusive rights to the mark. A trademark owner can block imported goods bearing a confusingly similar mark for the same type of good. If an owner must sue to enforce trademark rights and is successful against an infringer, the owner is entitled to injunctive relief (forcing the infringer to stop infringing), three times damages and the infringer's profits, together with legal expenses, in some circumstances.

 8. Register trademarks in your state if your product or service is limited to that state.

State registration may be sufficient if a product or service is not being offered or transported outside state boundaries. State registration provides benefits under that state's laws for use of the trademark only in that state. However, the protection provided by state registration may be weak or lost when another company with a similar mark, which is operating in multiple states (including your own), has a federal registration for its mark. Some states also provide for registration of a trade *name*, but many do not.

 9. Register trademarks early in foreign countries.

In many foreign countries, the right to exclusive use of a mark is based upon the first to file rather than the first to use, as in the United States. Thus if a trademark owner wishes to distribute its goods in another country, it should register the mark at the earliest possible moment, e.g., long before the goods are shipped. Some countries, such as Japan, do not provide service mark protection.

 10. Re the Internet: Perform a URL search to verify that a trademark is not already being used on the Web.

Many businesses are present on the World Wide Web by virtue

of a domain name or Uniform Resource Locator (URL). The domain name is both an address and a name, e.g., http://www.coke.com. Users placing a domain name on the Web which is confusingly similar to some company's registered mark have been prohibited from using the domain name. Recent court cases suggest that the use of domain names will be analyzed according to traditional principles of trademark and trade name law.

COPYRIGHTS

 11. Register your copyrighted material promptly with the United States Copyright Office.

Registration is required as a condition to bringing a lawsuit against an infringer in federal court under the federal Copyright Act. As with trademark protection, an owner is entitled to statutory damages and attorney fees if successful. Note: International copyright protection is a complex, specialized field that is outside the scope of this book.

 12. Require your employees to acknowledge in writing your company's copyright ownership and to assign to the company whatever interests the employee may have in any work being done.

Even in the traditional employer/employee relationship, a manager or owner is well served to deal with copyright ownership matters proactively. A contractor (who is not an employee) *must assign his or her copyright ownership and interests in their work.* Proceed with care when using assignments with non-employees. Some states require employers to notify contractors of certain rights provided under state statute.

13. *Always* state in writing who will own a copyright when more than one person or entity outside the typical employer/employee relationship contributes to a copyrighted work.

When non-employees get involved in the development of material there is great potential for misunderstanding that can result in litigation. Once again, the best prevention is to cover such matters early in a relationship. Independent contractors should be asked to provide written warranties stating that their work does not infringe upon the rights of others and agreeing to indemnify you against any damages which may occur as a result of a breach of the warranties.

 14. Establish and enforce policies that prohibit copying of materials which have a valid copyright by another person or entity.

Copying that is infringement is not limited to physical copying; it includes public distribution, display, use in a performance, and the preparation of derivative works. Copying is generally shown by proof of access to the materials and a fact of substantial similarity between the copyrighted work and the infringer's material.

Under the federal Copyright Act, fair use of copyrighted material is excepted from infringement. Fair use includes certain uses of copyrighted work for purposes like criticism, comment, news reporting, teaching, scholarship and research, and computer program back-up. The largest factor in determining whether use is "fair use" is whether the amount of material being used is disproportionately large and whether the fact of the borrowing is likely to have an adverse effect on sales of the original. If important to the whole, use of even a small amount of material can constitute infringement. When used in a for-profit (rather than a scholastic or personal) context, unauthorized use is likely to be infringing and not fair use.

15. Obtain permission before using any portion of a work copyrighted by others.

If there is any doubt about whether certain material is indeed copyrighted or whether the intended use meets the fair use exception to infringement, contact the author.

PATENTS

 16. Prepare in advance to file for a patent.

Inventors should document the development of their inventions in writing as they go along. It is also often useful to do a patentability search as early as possible in the process of invention. Employers should have in hand signed proprietary agreements with employees or others working with the company. Such agreements should confirm the signers' duty to assign the ownership of inventions to the company.

 17. File for a patent with the federal Patent and Trademark Office when you wish a patent and feel you have something new and useful that will qualify for a utility, design, or (organic) plant patent.

Obtaining a valid patent can be a time consuming and costly effort. However, it is the primary method to protect your invention. Any investment in such an effort should fit with the overall plans for building your company. Patent holders have a bundle of rights which they may transfer outright or by selling limited licenses. A patent license normally allows a non-exclusive or exclusive licensee to make, use and/or sell the invention in exchange for a lump sum payment, royalty payments, or both. Note: International patent protection is a complex and specialized subject that is outside the scope of this book. However, because most foreign countries do not have a one-year grace period for filing, you should file for a U.S. patent before any use, sale, or publication is made if you intend to seek foreign patents.

 18. When issued, place the patent number on the invention.

As with copyrighted material, a proper notice tells people in general that the invention is protected. This may avert innocent infringement defenses. If the notice is not used, the inventor may be prohibited from collecting damages from an infringer by a federal court.

GOODWILL

 19. Enter into a non-competition agreement (also known as a covenant not to compete) with key employees.

Although non-competition agreements are clearly a restraint of trade, most states will enforce such agreements if they are reasonable and supported by adequate consideration. Whether or not a non-competition agreement is reasonable usually depends on three factors. First, the **geographic area** in which the employee must not compete must be reasonable. For example, if your company distributes electronic marine supplies over a five-county area, it would be reasonable to prohibit an employee from competing in that area, but not the whole state. Nor would it be reasonable to prohibit an employee from competing twenty-five miles away in the suburbs if you have a dry-cleaning business that attracts customers in a downtown area.

Second, the time period in which an employee will not compete must be reasonable. While enforceable time periods vary from state to state and the particular circumstances, employers should generally not seek to restrict employment for more than three years. A particular employee's job responsibilities and access to information may determine the length of restriction. If the proprietary information known by the employee may change from year to year, such as pricing information, then a one-year restriction may be adequate and reasonable. If the employee has confidential information relating to a business's long-term goals, this fact might reasonably support a three-year limitation. Thus, a food manufacturer may be able to prohibit a managerial or supervisory employee who had access to a secret process or confidential business plan from competing for three years. But a production employee with limited knowledge of the process and no knowledge of the business plan might reasonably be prohibited for no more than three months, if at all.

Third, the type or **scope of activity** restricted must be reasonable. For example, a communications software development company may prohibit its employee (a software technician) from competing in the communications field with software he or she developed for the company, but the employee cannot be prohibited from working in a software company right next door that designs video games using a different technology.

 20. Implement policies regarding non-disclosure of confidential information and have key employees enter into non-disclosure agreements.

As goodwill includes confidential information and trade secrets developed by a company, it must be protected proactively. To keep secrets secret, mark materials appropriately, regulate access to them, and limit disclosure to third parties.

CONCLUSION

Intangible assets such as intellectual property (e.g., trademarks, patents) and proprietary information (e.g., customer lists) often constitute a significant part of the total value of a business. Protection of such assets is a continuing task. To stay out of court, owners and managers need to recognize relevant issues early even as they enact and enforce policies to maintain the legal integrity of their own organizations.

5

PRODUCT LIABILITY

"Humpty Dumpty may have had a case against the king."
–Anonymous

OVERVIEW

Essentially every product made is capable of causing, or at least being involved in, some form of personal injury or property damage. This means that companies that manufacture, wholesale, distribute and retail products have an exposure to claims for damages. Nowhere in business law is it more true that the best defense against such claims is a sound offense.

Product liability law consists of the unique set of rules covering the tort (non-contractual) claims associated with the manufacture and sale of products. For the most part, these rules apply uniformly to **everyone in the chain of distribution** of a product. For purposes of this chapter, these parties will be referred to collectively as *prod-*

uct sellers unless otherwise specified. Regardless of the number of tests conducted, precautions taken, or warnings given, product sellers have been and are the targets of injured parties seeking compensation for damages suffered.

There is little federal law that pertains to product liability. Most of the law that does exist is the result of state legislation and court decisions. Business people need to understand that the law relating to product liability varies widely from state to state. Moreover, the law relating to the preventive measures a product seller may take to avoid product liability also **varies widely from state to state**. And, in recent years, the courts and state legislatures have been revising the rules. Therefore, they are in flux. So, while the best defense against product liability claims is a sound offense, developing a sound offense and keeping it current is not a simple matter. In most companies, preventing product liability problems requires regular work with the employees and major systems of the enterprises.

THE LAW OF THE LAND

Typically the term, product liability, comes into play when personal injury or damage to property is caused by a defect in a product. Conversely, product liability generally does *not* cover those situations where a buyer of a product who has not suffered personal injuries or property damage seeks a refund or damages simply because the product did not meet expectations. This latter sort of claim is generally considered part of the law of sales rather than as part of the law of product liability. Most states have separate laws pertaining to sales; the laws are modeled after the Uniform Commercial Code (see Chapter 7 on Contracts).

There are three legal standards for recovery in the product liability law pertaining to personal injury or other damage:

Negligence by the product seller.
A product seller's breach of an express or implied warranty.
Strict liability.

Depending on the case, one or more of these legal standards will be used to determine the liability of a product seller whose defective product caused, or is alleged to have caused, injury.

Negligence of the Product Seller

To hold a product seller responsible for a defective product based on negligence, the injured party must prove that the product seller breached its **duty of care** to the injured party. This requires the injured party to show that the product seller or its employees did not exercise reasonable care for the safety of potential users of the product. For example, if an employee of a bicycle manufacturer fails to tightly secure the wheels on a particular bike, the manufacturer will be liable to the user who was subsequently injured when one or both of the wheels fell off. The manufacturer's **employee failed to exercise reasonable care.** There is no requirement that the injured party be the person who actually purchased the bicycle. It is sufficient that the injured person was a member of the reasonably foreseeable group of people who would use the product, in this case all potential riders of the bicycle.

Product Seller's Breach of Warranty

A breach of warranty claim arises when a product seller makes representations about what a product will do, but the product falls short on performance *and* causes injury. A warranty can either be *express* or *implied*. An express warranty is the written warranty which typically accompanies a product when it is sold or which is contained in the contract for sale of the product. **An express warranty can also be created by representations made by the product seller to promote the product.** Such representations often show up in advertising or promotional materials. A product must live up to the representations made for it.

An *implied* warranty is different. It is not initiated by the product seller; it is a product of our legal system, a part of the law of the land. The most common type is the implied warranty of merchantability which covers all goods. It means that any given product is warranted to be of a quality equal to that generally acceptable among those who deal in similar goods, and that the product is generally fit for the ordinary purposes for which such product is used.

Many states have limited the use of the breach of warranty, express or implied, to claims involving contracts for the sale of goods in which the buyer has suffered commercial economic losses. This means an injured party can bring a claim for breach of warranty *only* if she or he had entered into a contract for the sale of goods with the product seller, the warranty associated with the contract was breached, and the buyer suffered commercial economic damage thereby.

A related rule adopted by a majority of states is that a buyer who suffers only economic damage as a result of a defective product may bring a claim against the product seller only if he or she purchased the defective product pursuant to a sales contract. In other words, the product cannot have been simply purchased off the shelf.

Strict Liability

Generally all an injured party must show to hold a product seller liable under the strict liability standard is (1) that the product was defective at the time the product seller transferred the product, and (2) that the defect caused the injured party's injuries. A minority of states also require the injured party to demonstrate that an alternative design for the product existed which would have prevented his or her injuries.

Strict liability offers many advantages to claimants over both the negligence and breach of warranty standards. Unlike the negligence standard, the injured party does not have to prove that the product seller or its employees acted without due care. Under the strict liability standard **it is no defense that the product seller exercises all possible care.** If the product was defective when delivered, the product seller is liable for any injuries caused, regardless of the precautions taken by the seller to prevent injury. And, unlike the breach of warranty standard, **it is no defense to a strict liability claim that there was no contractual relationship between the product seller and the injured party.** For example, in the case of the bicycle manufacturer mentioned earlier, suppose a person walking down the street is injured when a bicycle careens into him or her because it lost a wheel due to a defect. That person could sue the manufacturer even though no contractual relationship existed between the two.

In most states, all three standards for liability apply to all product sellers, i.e., once again, to everyone in the chain of distribution—manufacturers, wholesalers, distributors, and retailers. Because of the severity of the strict liability standard, however, a few states have limited its applicability to manufacturers only. In such states, retailers, for example, are only liable for negligence or breach of warranty claims.

TYPES OF DEFECTS

Before any of the above legal standards can be employed, an injured party must first prove that the product which caused her or his injuries was defective. There can be no valid product liability claim without proof of the presence of a defective product whether the action is based on negligence, breach of warranty, or strict liability. There are three common types of defects which can support a product liability claim: construction defects, design defects, and warning or instruction defects.

Construction Defects

A construction defect occurs when the product deviates in some material way from the design specifications or performance standards of the manufacturer. In other words, the product is different in some material way from otherwise identical units off the same production line. For example, suppose the automatic shut-off mechanism (to prevent over-heating) was missing on a laundry iron manufactured by Company A. The defective iron caused a fire. Upon investigation it turns out that the problem occurred because a person who was responsible for installing the shut-off device made a mistake. This is a construction defect. The iron is designed properly; it was put together with a defect. It did not contain the automatic shut-off device that the other irons coming off the production line possessed.

Design Defects

A design defect occurs when the product is not reasonably safe as designed. Here is a working definition of reasonably safe:

A product is not reasonably safe as designed...if the risk of harm plus the seriousness of the harm...is greater than the burden on the manufacturer of designing a product without the risk plus the adverse effect the new design would have on the product's performance.

This definition is virtually identical to that contained in the Model Uniform Product Liability Act published by the Department of Commerce for *voluntary* use by states. Said more simply: **A design defect results when the benefits of the design are outweighed by its risks!** The expectations of the ordinary consumer need to be taken into account when making this determination.

Here is an example. A manufacturer of automatic coffee makers could produce its coffee makers less expensively than it does if it used a lower grade of plastic to house the heating element. The risk, however, is that such plastic melts under certain conditions of use. Although a cheaper coffee maker might meet the expectations of many consumers, the harm potentially caused by such a product may outweigh the cost of using the higher grade of plastic and the added cost to the consumer. Many courts would say so. A coffee maker made with a low grade of plastic would be held to have a design defect.

Although a design defect closely resembles a negligence standard, most courts hold that a design defect is generally easier to prove than negligence.

Warning or Instruction Defects

A warning or instruction defect arises when the likelihood that a product will cause harm or injury, plus the seriousness thereof, render the warnings or instructions actually provided to be inadequate. Like a design defect, these defects resemble a negligence standard. However, many **courts have held that a product seller may be liable for inadequate warnings even though the hazard was not known at the time of manufacture.** Moreover, some states require product sellers to issue warnings or instructions concerning dangers that are learned, **or should be learned,** after products are manufactured.

> *CASE C: In the early evening of September 22, 1996, 15-month old David Smith and his twin brother were playing in their parents' house. David entered a bedroom where he found an open purse belonging to his 13-year old sister, Laurie, on the floor. Inside the purse was an unmarked container that Laurie had filled with Company C's baby oil. David's mother unexpectedly came across David just as he began to drink the oil. In an immediate and concerned reaction, she yelled at David to stop, causing him to gasp and inhale some of the oil into his lungs. Had David simply drunk the oil, the only effect would have been diarrhea. Instead, the oil diffused throughout David's lungs, reducing their ability to deliver oxygen to his blood. As a result, David suffered irreparable brain damage. David's parents brought a product liability action against Company C based on a failure to warn of the danger of aspirating (inhaling) baby oil. At the trial, expert testimony established that no amount of medical attention would have prevented David's injuries. No similar incident had ever occurred in the past.*

In Case C, the court held that the warnings provided on the original bottle were inadequate and therefore defective even though the hazard of aspirating baby oil was not known at the time of manufacture. Then the court held further that Company C was strictly liable for David's injuries. No showing of foreseeability was necessary because the strict liability standard was employed.

In summary, for product liability there are three standards—negligence, breach of warranty, and strict liability. And there are three types of defects—construction, design, and warning or instruction—that can set the stage for one of the standards to apply in a given situation.

HOW TO MINIMIZE
YOUR LEGAL TROUBLES

The development of the strict liability standard makes it quite difficult for a product seller to defend itself successfully against a product liability claim. Nonetheless, a number of affirmative steps can be taken by a product seller to help minimize its exposure to product liability claims.

 1. Take all necessary steps to prevent the shipment of defective products.

If there is no defective product, there can be no successful product liability claim!

 2. Continuously test and update designs, quality measures, and warnings in order to anticipate product problems.

In many cases, lack of foreseeability (of a danger) is no longer a viable defense against a product liability claim. Therefore, it is imperative for a product seller to take the initiative to identify hazards before they harm someone or property. Once an injury occurs, it is too late.

 3. Conduct training for employees.

A product seller should periodically discuss product liability exposure and its implications to the enterprise as part of an overall, on-going effort to insure that people know how to do their jobs properly. Keep the issue of minimizing product liability exposure in the company philosophy, from design to manufacturing.

4. Maintain accurate records.

Product liability claims often arise years after a product was designed and delivered. It is not unusual for the people most knowledgeable about the details to be gone from the company. In such cases, written records become the primary source of evidence. Product sellers need to have a system for generating and retaining documents which are likely to be useful if there is ever a product liability claim.

5. Be careful what you say to promote your products.

Statements made in ads and other sales materials or in the selling process itself can be construed by a court as express warranties. For instance, an automobile salesperson who says to a potential customer, "mother nature can't stir up a snow storm nasty enough to prevent this four-wheel drive vehicle from getting over the pass," may be warranting the same. The seller could be held liable for the buyer's injuries when he or she is subsequently involved in an accident while driving over a pass (testing the seller's warranty). It is important to examine all promotional activities for inadvertent representations about what a product will or will not do.

6. Make disclaimers.

A product seller can explicitly disclaim or limit its liability for defects in the product. For example, the seller of a high-powered paint sprayer could disclaim any liability for damage caused to a buyer's property by paint that is oversprayed. Such disclaimers must be conspicuously visible in writing, and in some states they must be explicitly negotiated with buyers in the context of a sales agreement. Although **contractual disclaimers will not prevent a consumer from recovering for personal injuries,** they can act to bar claims for property damage and commercial loss. The requirements for creating a valid disclaimer are complex.

7. Specify the useful life of the product.

The useful life of a product should be specified somewhere on the product, its packaging, or in the contract of sale. As a general rule, a product seller cannot be subject to liability **if the harm caused by a product occurred after the product's, specified useful life.** A useful life extends from the time of delivery through the time during which the product would normally be likely to perform if put to productive use. "Time of delivery" refers to delivery to the end user, i.e., the first purchaser who is not engaged in the business of either re-selling the product or using it as a component part of another product to be sold. In many states, there is a presumption that after a period of years, ten, for example, any harm caused was after the useful safe life of the subject product.

8. Heed government mandates.

In many states, if at the time of manufacture a given product was in compliance with a specific mandatory government contract specification relating to the design or warnings, such compliance will be an absolute defense to liability. Similarly, the fact that a product was in compliance with industry customs and other regulatory standards may be taken into account positively in determining a product seller's liability.

The above eight steps constitute the basic elements of the sound offense advocated at the start of this chapter. The final step to minimizing legal troubles occurs in connection with a claim that is threatened or has been filed.

 9. Check your state's statute of limitations.

A claim may be barred by an applicable statute of limitations. Such statutes impose deadlines beyond which an injured party may not bring an action. The deadlines typically range from one to six years. For negligence and strict liability claims, the statute begins to run from the day a person is injured. In many states, however, the statute does not begin to run until the injured party discovers, or reasonably should have discovered, all the elements of her or his cause of action.

CONCLUSION

Product liability is a hot topic these days, and many business people warm up quickly when the subject is raised. Damage settlements with huge penalties against companies seem to regularly make the headlines. Laws and courts vary greatly from state to state. And there have been well-publicized attempts to modify tort law at the federal level in recent years. The bottom line, however, is that product sellers remain responsible for their products and what they do. The cost of losing a product liability suit can be more than just a cost of doing business. It can be the business itself. The essence of the action steps above are, for the most part, simply good management. Vigilance is required.

6

UNFAIR BUSINESS
&
TRADE PRACTICES

*"Industry can be saved only by itself;
competition is its life."*

–Balzac (1833)

OVERVIEW

To be in business is to compete. To win in business is to outdo competitors in terms of attracting, serving, and keeping customers. Just *how* companies go about outdoing competitors is today a subject of public policy, however.

Near the end of the nineteenth century, economic activity in the United States had become dominated by cartels (small groups of competitors acting in concert), monopolies (single companies able to control markets), and trusts (financial companies which effectively controlled the major competitors in a given industry). In those days, economic power was essentially concentrated in the hands of a relatively small number of individuals. In general, they won and consumers lost.

In response to growing concerns across the country about excessive prices and unfair competition, in 1890 Congress passed the first of many antitrust measures. It was then, and is still, laudatory to win in business, but there are rules about how an enterprise must compete, and there are limits on how much economic power can be accumulated by one or a small number of companies. These rules, laws, are the products of both the federal and state governments.

THE LAW OF THE LAND

There are two primary concerns addressed by the law. The first is consumer protection, law to shield consumers from unfair or deceptive business practices. The second is antitrust, law that prohibits unfair methods of competition between businesses, i.e., activities which actually decrease the overall intensity of competition.

Consumer Protection

The basic purpose of consumer protection law is to prohibit sharp practices and dishonest dealing in consumer transactions. The FTC (Federal Trade Commission) Act is the primary federal statute prohibiting unfair or deceptive business practices with respect to the consumer. Virtually every state has passed legislation modeled after the FTC Act in which *unfair or deceptive acts or practices in or affecting commerce are declared unlawful.* An act or practice can violate a consumer protection law if it is unfair *or* deceptive. It does not have to be both!

The FTC enforces federal consumer law either through an administrative complaint tried before an administrative law judge or through actions for preliminary injunctions, consumer redress, and civil penalties brought in a federal district court. The FTC may issue a **cease and desist** order against an offending business, and it may impose substantial penalties for violations of that order. Private individuals or corporations may not sue under the Act. However, under state consumer protection law, both states' attorneys general and private, aggrieved parties may bring an action for violation of the law. Private parties, like an attorney general, can typically seek injunctive relief to enjoin or prevent the improper practice, and they can seek payment for damages caused by the practice. State laws directed against unfair or deceptive acts or practices also often allow punitive damages and provide for the award of attorneys fees.

What does "unfair" or "deceptive" mean? The FTC's **definition of unfair** provides the following criteria:

(1) whether the practice, without necessarily having been previously considered unlawful, offends public policy as it has been established by statutes, common law or otherwise — whether, in other words, it is within at least the penumbra of some common-law, statutory or other established concept of unfairness;
(2) whether it is immoral, unethical, oppressive or unscrupulous; and
(3) whether it causes substantial injury to consumers (or competitors or other businesses).

The FTC considers an act or practice deceptive if (1) there is a representation, omission, or practice that (2) is likely to mislead consumers acting reasonably under the circumstances, and (3) the representation, omission, or practice is material. Some states have established a broader definition of what is deceptive in that they prohibit conduct that has the "capacity to deceive."

Clearly an act or practice that is unfair or deceptive and that a company knowingly engages in to increase sales or to beat its competitors will constitute a violation of consumer protection law. Here is a case to illustrate how a company might end up engaging in a deceptive practice without necessarily intending to do so.

> *CASE D: Company D manufactures vacuum cleaners. The company is organized in three divisions: Design, Manufacturing, and Marketing & Sales. Company D has a new product that is scheduled to be shipped to retail stores by a certain date. Marketing & Sales developed promotional material based on the original, new design. In part, the material says that the new vacuum cleaner is "powered by a more powerful motor exclusively manufactured for Company D by Company X, a U.S. Company." It also says "all parts are made in the USA." Shortly before the new product is shipped, Company X encounters difficulties and Company D people quickly find a Canadian company to supply the needed motors which are installed in the new product.*
>
> *Marketing & Sales are not told of the substitution; therefore, no change is made in the promotional material and it is used in the field.*

This practice would likely constitute a deceptive act or practice by Company D to the extent that the misrepresentations in the promotional materials are deemed to be "material" under the definition above.

Following are some other examples of actual practices that have been found to be **unfair** under the FTC definitions:

- Taking a customer's car to evaluate for trade-in purposes and then refusing to return the car until the customer purchases a car.
- Delivering an incorrect mobile home to a home site and refusing to remove it from the purchaser's property.
- Substituting building materials that do not conform to the requirements specified in a contract.

And here are some actual practices found to be **deceptive** under the definitions used above:

- Telling a customer that insurance is required when it really isn't.
- Misrepresenting the terms of a written sales contract.
- Using misleading opinions or statements about the economic potential of an investment.
- Attracting customers with product A and then switching them to another product, B. ("Bait and Switch.")
- Failing to warn a physician of known risks associated with a drug. (Deception by a pharmaceutical company.)

It is important to recognize that lawmakers at both the federal and state levels have deliberately refused to define *all* prohibited practices. They appreciate that there is no limit to human inventiveness! So the law concerning what is unfair and deceptive evolves over time.

Antitrust

The basic purpose of antitrust law is to promote free enterprise and open competition that leads to low prices and better products in the marketplace. The intent is to prohibit the concentration of economic power. The **Sherman Act** of 1890 and the additional federal and state legislation that has followed it over the years provide the rules that govern business competition in the United States today.

Section 1 of the Sherman Act contains a basic prohibition against the collaborative actions of two or more persons in restraint of trade. The Act states that *every contract, combination in the form of trust or otherwise, or conspiracy, in restraint of trade or commerce among the several States, or with foreign nations, is declared to be illegal.* Violators are guilty of a felony and subject to criminal sanctions including fines and imprisonment. Section 3 of the Act extends the prohibition to District of Columbia and all U.S. territories.

In the literal sense, **virtually every contract made between companies includes some element that restrains trade.** For example, a business might contract to buy parts at a favorable price and therefore cut off bids from other suppliers. However, the Supreme Court has construed Section 1 to apply to contracts and combinations which constitute *unreasonable* restraints of trade. Unless a particular restraint falls within a category that has already been judicially disapproved, the restraint will be tested for reasonableness.

Section 2 of the Sherman Act contains a basic prohibition against undue concentrations of economic power. The Act states that *every person who shall monopolize, or attempt to monopolize, or combine or conspire with any other person or persons, to monopolize any part of the trade or commerce among the several States, or with foreign nations, shall be deemed guilty of a felony...* **Violators are subject to criminal sanctions.** Section 2 applies to both the unilateral actions of a single entity, as well as to collaborative actions of two or more entities.

The **Clayton Act** was adopted in 1914 to specifically prohibit some of the business practices that continued after the passage of the Sherman Act. Section 3 of the Clayton Act deals with simple exclusive dealing arrangements, as well as arrangements tying separate products together for sale. Section 7 of the Act prohibits acquisitions where *the effect of such acquisition may be substantially to lessen competition or tend to create a monopoly.* As amended and strengthened by the Robinson-Patman Act in 1936, Section 2 of the Clayton Act prohibits price discrimination between purchasers.

Finally, the FTC Act prohibits *unfair methods of competition in or affecting commerce, and unfair or deceptive acts or practices in or affecting commerce.*

The most important federal antitrust statutes are covered above. These statutes are aimed at maintaining strict competition within interstate commerce and commerce with foreign nations. In order to address business practices of commerce within a state's borders, most states have also adopted their own antitrust laws. Some of these laws resemble the Sherman Act and other federal legislation.

In summary to this point, the law of the land is aimed at consumer protection and maximizing competition between companies. There are federal laws that apply; many states have additional laws to fill in gaps or enhance consumer protection and business competition.

TYPES OF CLAIMS

There are somewhat different procedures for the two areas.

Consumer Protection

As indicated earlier, the FTC enforces federal law either through an administrative complaint tried before an administrative law judge or through actions for preliminary injunctions, consumer redress, and civil actions brought in a federal district court. State law allows both attorneys general and private parties to initiate actions in the state court system.

Antitrust

Antitrust claims can either target the actions of an individual competitor or the collaborative actions of multiple competitors. Depending on the particular violation, offenders may be subject to civil penalties, or they may trigger criminal prosecution. In practice, crimes that are either hard to detect or financially lucrative are more likely to attract the attention of criminal prosecutors. Such crimes can lead to the harsher sanction of criminal penalties.

In a civil (non-criminal) prosecution, the federal government may obtain an injunction prohibiting the continuation of specific business activities; it may also obtain damages for injury to a business or property. Except as otherwise provided in the FTC Act, civil enforcement of federal antitrust laws is shared between the Department of Justice and the FTC.

Federal antitrust law also empowers private persons or entities (rather than the FTC or the Justice Department) to bring their own civil lawsuits for damages caused by antitrust violations. Remedies available to private parties include triple damages, injunctions, court costs, and attorney fees. Private suits are permitted to proceed without regard for the status of any concurrent governmental action, even if both suits address substantially the same allegations of misconduct.

For criminal prosecutions, the Department of Justice's Antitrust Division has exclusive responsibility. The attorney general may elect to bring a criminal suit against a defendant, even if a civil suit addressing the very same activity resulted in no liability for the same defendant. In addition to injunctions and damages, a federal criminal prosecution may result in criminal sanctions, including both fines and imprisonment. In the case of a corporate defendant, directors and officers may be subject to imprisonment if their actions violate the antitrust statutes.

For example, the two largest billboard companies in California entered into an agreement in 1964 whereby each agreed not to bid on the other's billboard sites for a period of one year following the termination of a lease on a given site. Although the explicit agreement was terminated in 1969, both companies continued to honor the agreement for an additional 15 years. When their practices were discovered, criminal charges were brought against the senior executives as well as the companies.

AGREEMENTS BETWEEN COMPETITORS

Most agreements between or among competitors that have an unreasonable negative effect upon competition are unlawful. Even if the primary purpose of the agreement is completely unrelated to suppressing competition, courts are likely to invalidate such an agreement if competition is unreasonably restricted. In addition, there are certain types of agreements which are almost *always* found to be unreasonable and, thereby, invalid by the courts. They include:

Price Fixing

Price fixing is a conspiracy among two or more competitors to stabilize or tamper with prices. Such efforts are conclusively prohibited under federal antitrust law, even in cases where the price ultimately settled upon was reasonable. Price agreements between side-by-side competitors (horizontal fixing) are illegal; courts have also prohibited agreements between buyers and sellers to fix resale prices (vertical fixing). However, manufacturers are usually permitted to supply their distributors with a list of suggested retail prices so long as the dealers are allowed to independently set their own final prices. Price fixing is illegal regardless of whether prices are raised or lowered. Even the mere exchange of pricing information among competitors may be prohibited if it has the effect of stabilizing prices.

CASE E: A state association of licensed real estate appraisers published a fee schedule recommending minimum fees to be charged for the appraisals buyers of real property needed to obtain financing. Research showed that the fees actually charged by the real estate appraisers across the state were nearly always equal to or above the recommended minimum fee on the schedule. In fact, the state association periodically disciplined members who charged less than the minimum fee. The FTC challenged this pricing practice by the association. The association answered that it was merely disseminating information about past practices. The court held that the association was fixing a minimum price for appraisals in violation of Section 1 of the Sherman Act.

Market or Customer Allocation

Agreements between side-by-side ("horizontal") competitors to divide up customers, territories, or markets are illegal. The prohibition against allocating customers applies even when the competitors are not yet in actual competition, and even when the competitors do not dominate the industry. Horizontal allocations are illegal regardless of the impact on prices, if any.

In contrast, agreements between sellers and buyers are not automatically illegal unless it includes an element of price fixing. Such "vertical" restraints of trade are usually tested for reasonableness. Case F illustrates the point.

CASE F: A brewer of beer imposed territorial marketing restrictions on its distributors. Wholesalers were assigned territories for authorized distribution of the beer, and they were not allowed to sell to retailers outside their assigned territories. One wholesaler challenged the arrangement in court. Since no price restrictions were involved, the court assessed the legality of the restrictions by looking for unreasonable anti-competitive impacts in the geographic market. The court found that the vertical restraints did not have an unreasonable negative impact on competition. They were, therefore, legal in this case.

Other Agreements

Business transactions which unreasonably restrain trade are unlawful under the Sherman Act. Unless certain practices and agreements have already been examined and held to be illegal, they will be assessed by the court as to reasonableness. In general, many practices and agreements have passed the antitrust test, either because of a minimal effect on competition or because other factors outweighed the negative effect on competition. For example, many businesses are bought and sold subject to the seller's agreement not to open a competing business for a certain length of time. Similarly, many employment contracts include non-compete elements (see Chapter 3). So long as such arrangements have a legitimate business purpose, they may be enforceable despite some anti-competitiveness effect.

UNILATERAL ANTI-COMPETITIVE ACTIONS

In addition to the agreements between competitors discussed above, certain anti-competitive strategies have been outlawed in cases where only one enterprise is involved.

Tying Arrangements

A tying arrangement occurs when a party makes the sale of one product to a buyer conditional upon the purchase of another, separate product. If the seller has sufficient market power to force the purchaser to buy an unwanted, additional product, then the seller's actions are automatically illegal. The effect of such an arrangement is to restrict competition in the market.

Monopolization

Monopoly power is the power to control prices or exclude competitors from a market. Actual monopolization is prohibited by the Sherman Act. It is defined as the willful acquisition or maintenance of monopoly power in a relevant market. Attempts to monopolize, for example through the acquisition of competitors, are also prohibited. If monopoly power is achieved through growth or development resulting from superior products, business acumen, or accident, there is no violation. For example, patents allow innovative people and producers to legally enjoy significant market power during the life of the patent.

Monopoly power has to do with control over prices and competitors. It is not necessary that a company have 100% of sales, or anywhere near 100% in a particular market, in order for it to have monopoly power. Generally, companies with less than 50% market share have been found to *lack* monopoly power, even if they have a larger share of the market than any other competitor. But if such a company has the power to control prices or exclude competitors, it does have monopoly power, regardless of its market share.

Price Discrimination

Price discrimination occurs when a seller discriminates in price between different purchasers of products of like grade and quality. The **Robinson-Patman** Act is intended to prevent economically powerful companies from obtaining favorable prices that are withheld from weaker companies in the same industry. Sellers are permitted to quote a lower price for quantity purchases, but the lower price must be based upon real cost savings and be available to all buyers on equal terms.

HOW TO MINIMIZE YOUR LEGAL TROUBLES

It is useful to keep in mind the basic purposes of the law covered in this chapter, namely, the protection of consumers and the promotion of competition. With these purposes in mind, common sense and normal professional management practices will do a lot to help you stay out of court and in business.

CONSUMER PROTECTION

 1. Monitor all aspects of your marketing and sales effort including advertising, product literature, and sales tactics.

Are you saying things that are misleading to consumers? Do you promise more than you know your product or service can deliver? Do you or your people withhold information that would be material to a consumer's decision whether or not to buy? (There are also product liability considerations in connection with claims you or your marketing and sales people make about your products or services. See Chapter 5.)

 2. Listen to your customers.

Address customer complaints promptly. If they say your product is not performing as advertised, for example, pay attention. Complaints can be a handy "red flag" for possible consumer litigation.

3. Familiarize your key people—particularly your sales management—with the contents of this chapter.

There are an increasing number of consumer protection claims, federal and state, brought against companies by private individuals. In fact, consumer protection has become a big business. For a company, the best preventive action against such claims is an informed workforce and a management team committed to doing what is best for the customers of the enterprise.

ANTITRUST

 4. Avoid making agreements with competitors. Any action which impedes the operation of free competition in your marketplace is potentially illegal.

Even sharing information with competitors can be risky. And most certainly agreements or activities which have the ultimate effect of stabilizing prices are prime targets for legal initiatives.

 5. Review acquisitions carefully in advance.

Some companies grow by buying other companies. Such acquisitions usually do not violate antitrust laws. But the question should be asked in the search process: Would this purchase significantly reduce competition? If the answer is "yes," or, "maybe," you may be forced to defend your actions.

 6. Focus your business on beating competition within the rules.

Develop and sell superior products; build a company that excels in application expertise or some other form of service; or be outstanding in your choice of locations and/or other conveniences. Being the best at your particular business does not itself constitute a violation of the law.

CONCLUSION

Commerce plays a leading role in our society. For people in business this is the good news. The accompanying bad news is that the burdens—strings attached—on those in leading roles are greater than on those in lesser roles. *Caveat emptor*, buyer beware, was once the prevailing sentiment across the land. Over the years since the FTC Act and many state consumer protection acts, this motto has been gradually abandoned. Today it is *caveat company*. Federal and state law requires honest, open dealing by an enterprise with both its consumers and its competitors.

Stay Out of Court and In Business

7

CONTRACTS

"A piece of paper blown by the wind into a law court may in the end only be drawn out again by two oxen."
-Chinese Proverb, S.G. Champion, 1938

OVERVIEW

Simply defined, a contract is a form of promise that is legally enforceable. Such promises are essential to trade and commerce. Every day people in business make and receive commitments. Contracts are expressions of those commitments. They provide the basis for planning. Companies enter contracts to lease space, purchase parts, deliver services on time, hire key people, transport goods, and so on. Contracts are central to building a business, any business. They give managers a level of certainty upon which to proceed. In a business context, the primary purpose of contracts is to protect the commercially reasonable expectations of the parties involved. All promises are not legally enforceable. Only some are. To rise to the level of being a contract, a promise must meet certain requirements. Building a business is easier when people understand those requirements and are comfortable with them. Such understanding includes an appreciation of the ramifications of a breach or default under a contract, the source of much litigation.

THE LAW OF THE LAND

Although courts throughout the country vary somewhat in the specific language they use to define a contract, any contract definition would typically incorporate the following essential elements: A contract is...

One or more promises with regard to which the law imposes a duty to perform and for the breach of which the law provides a remedy.

The promise that provides the basic element of a given contract typically starts as an offer or proposal to do something or to refrain from doing something. The offer or proposal may be in writing or it may be made orally. In either case, it must reflect an intent to enter into and become bound by a contract; it must be more than mere discussion about possible arrangements.

In the U.S.A. the law of contracts is derived from court decisions, generally referred to as common law, and from statutes, i.e., laws passed by legislatures. The primary statutory reference on contracts is the U.C.C. (Uniform Commercial Code) which has been adopted in virtually all jurisdictions. The U.C.C. was created to bring about a degree of uniformity among American jurisdictions. The first version of the U.C.C. was published in 1951; there have been several revisions since then. While different states have adopted different versions and added their own variations, the general principles and concepts of the U.C.C. are similar from state to state. The U.C.C. covers the sale of goods and a number of other topics including promissory notes and other commercial paper, bills of lading, and personal property secured transactions, that is, the granting of security interest in personal property to secure payment of a debt.

ELEMENTS OF A CONTRACT

To be valid, a contract must have two essential elements. They are as follows:

1. There must be an offer and an acceptance between designated parties to do or not do something specific.
-The parties involved must be identified.
-The subject of the contract must be specified,
   e.g., the goods, services, or actions.
-The time of performance must be stated or implied.

2. There must be consideration between the parties involved.

We will examine these two elements, offer and acceptance, and consideration, one at a time.

Offer and Acceptance

The starting point in the making of a contract is an offer by a specific party to do or not do something specific. Once an offer has been extended, it must be accepted by a specific party prior to any revocation or termination. As a general rule, offers are revocable at any time with a few exceptions. An offer can include a fixed maturity date after which it is revoked. Under common (court-made) law, an offer might be irrevocable if the recipient paid something to keep the offer open. Also, under common law, an offer might be deemed to be open if the recipient "detrimentally relied" on the offer, provided such reliance was reasonable and foreseeable to the offeror. Even in these circumstances, if there is no fixed maturity, courts will generally treat the offer as only being open for a reasonable time.

When an offer is accepted, it must be accepted in an unequivocal and unqualified manner. Prior to the use of electronic communication—facsimile, email—a substantial body of common law evolved from court decisions dealing with acceptances and revocations for concurrent offers that passed each other in the mail. There may in some circumstances still be relevance to this common law, but today much of it is moot.

If the stated acceptance of a given offer is qualified or if it includes an attempt to change the terms and conditions of the offer, then under common law the acceptance is treated as a **counteroffer.** This means the acceptance merely has the legal effect of rejecting the original offer! Once rejected, the original offer is automatically revoked and cannot be reinstated unless the offeror is willing to do so. While "mere inquiries" concerning possible changes in terms and conditions in the original offer might not be viewed as a counteroffer, such inquiries are best made with caution where the intent is probably to accept the offer as made.

In transactions between merchants, the U.C.C. creates an exception to the requirement for an unconditional, unqualified acceptance. As a general proposition, in this exception, additional terms proposed in an acceptance by the recipient (offeree) may create a contract, with the additional terms becoming part of the contract if they do not materially alter the original offer and are not rejected by the offeror. Otherwise, they are excluded from the contract.

Unfortunately, the salutary purpose of this provision of the U.C.C. is undercut by further provisions permitting the offeror to limit acceptance to the terms of the original offer and permitting the offeree to condition acceptance to its additional terms. This has generally led to the **battle of the forms** in which each party endeavors to impose its own terms and conditions on the other. Case G outlines such a battle.

CASE G: Company G orders certain goods from Company B by sending a purchase order to B. The purchase order form contains, on the back in fine print, a requirement that the goods shall be warranted free of defects for a period of six months and that the offer to buy can only be accepted in accordance with the stated terms. Company B receives the P.O. and sends G an order "acceptance" form. It contains, on the back in fine print, a statement that all goods are sold with a 90-day warranty and that the acceptance is expressly made conditional on the purchaser's agreement to these terms of sale.

This acceptance by B would likely be considered by a court to be a material alteration to the orginal offer to buy. However, no one at Company G (or B) reads the terms on the backs of the forms.

B ships the goods; after five months they develop a defect. There is a dispute between the two companies. Resolution of the matter will depend upon which company's terms prevail and what supplementary terms may be incorporated under provisions of the U.C.C.

Case G is an example of the battle of the forms. In such a situation, it is uncertain which party would prevail if the matter ends up in court.

In many situations, offer and acceptance is accomplished by an exchange of promises, that is, an offer to sell is accepted by an offer to buy and pay. However, it is not uncommon for an offer to be accepted by performance. This might occur, for example, where an order is placed for so many units of a particular product, at a specified price, to be delivered by a specified date. The recipient might accept by sending a confirmation, a promise to do an act in the future, but it might also accept by proceeding to deliver the goods. Obviously, if a manager is striving for certainty, which is a primary reason for contracts, then it would be preferable in most instances to obtain an **acceptance by a promise to perform,** rather than await performance, particularly if it is to occur at some distant date. Moreover, in such circumstances the recipient of the offer might also want to accept by a promise rather than performance, to avoid the possibility of the offeror later wanting to revoke the offer.

As indicated earlier, the promises that make up a contract can be either written or oral. In most situations, a written contract is preferable because of the greater certainty of terms. However, **an oral promise can often result in a binding contract.** While many states have enacted Statutes of Frauds that *require* certain contracts to be in writing, the subject matter of the contracts included within these Statutes is rather limited. For businesses, they typically include contracts whose performance goes beyond one year, guarantees of another person's debt, and contracts for the purchase or sale of real property.

Also, under the U.C.C., contracts for the sale of goods above a certain minimum price must be in writing. The figure of $500 is specified in the basic U.C.C. text, but this number varies from state to state. **As a basic rule, business people looking for certainty will wisely use a written contract for anything essential to building and running their businesses.** If an oral contract is within the Statute of Frauds, where there has been some partial performance, the courts may examine the nature and extent of that performance to determine whether it is sufficient to remove that oral contract from the Statute. The results of such an examination are difficult to predict.

Even when parties enter into a written contract, questions often arise about the impact of other written or oral agreements entered into either previously or at the same time. A substantive rule of law, commonly referred to as the Parole Evidence Rule, states that where parties have agreed to a written instrument as a complete and final expression of their contract, *extrinsic* evidence—that is, evidence of matters not contained in the instrument—of prior or contemporaneous agreements (written or oral) is *not* admissible to vary or add to the terms of that writing.

However, in practice, this Rule does not provide easy resolution to many disputes. Whether the written contract is a complete and final expression, i.e., integrated, sometimes ends up as a matter for a court to decide. A court does this by looking at the agreement itself; it may also consider outside, extrinsic, evidence on the question of the parties' intents. In an attempt to avoid this potential problem, parties to a contract often add an "integration" or "merger" clause. It expressly states that the contract is the final agreement of the parties and supersedes all prior and contemporaneous discussions, understandings, and agreements. This can be helpful although it is not always the final word.

If a court determines that the written agreement in question is not integrated, the evidence of the other agreements is admissible. However, whether or not such other agreements are actually treated as part of the contract remains a question of fact to be argued by the parties and decided by the court.

The Parole Evidence Rule is not a complete bar to the consideration of extrinsic evidence, even if the written agreement is determined to have integration. For example, if the language of a particular, written contract is ambiguous, the extrinsic evidence may be admissible to help explain the language. Further, extrinsic evidence may be admissible to show fraud, duress, mistake, or to establish a collateral agreement that does not contradict the integrated agreement and whose subject is so distinct that it might reasonably be excluded from the integrated agreement. These issues become particularly complicated and indicate the importance of having a written agreement that includes *all* the relevant terms or that specifically references and incorporates terms contained in other documents.

Consideration

There must be value given by each party to a contract in order to make it enforceable. To put it more bluntly, **in order to get something you have to give up something.** This is the underlying legal prerequisite for every contract. Without consideration from all the parties involved, there is no contract, i.e., legally enforceable promise. Promises to make a gift are unenforceable; promises based upon consideration previously received are unenforceable; contracts based upon such concepts as moral duty are unenforceable. In short, and subject to very few exceptions, a mere promise without value exchanged does not make a contract.

While consideration is a basic prerequisite for a contract, our courts generally will *not* scrutinize the **amount of consideration** to determine whether what is given up by each party is equivalent. However, more than nominal value must be given.

Questions often arise in a business setting about promises that may be quite illusory or lack mutuality of obligation. If there is not a definite commitment to do certain acts or to incur a certain legal obligation, such promises may on their face appear to lack mutuality of obligation, *but courts may, nevertheless, imply an obligation.*

Courts in some situations imply an obligation to use "reasonable efforts" or "best efforts." For example, this could be the case in a distributorship agreement where a representative has been given an exclusive territory without an express performance requirement or standard.

Or, as another example, companies may enter into "requirement" or "output" contracts. A company may agree to buy its requirements of coal during a given winter from a particular supplier in return for a set price. While in theory the purchaser has not obligated itself to buy any particular amount of coal—which might suggest that the contract is illusory—the contract is nevertheless enforceable since the commitment or legal detriment to the purchaser is to buy the coal it needs, if it needs any, from that particular supplier.

While consideration is a key element to a contract, there are exceptions. The most notable one is the Doctrine of Promissory Estoppel under which **a court will enforce a promise,** even if gratuitously made, if action by the receiving party in justifiable reliance on that promise was *reasonably foreseeable* and the receiving party incurred substantial economic detriment. However, a court might limit the enforcement of the original promise only to the extent necessary to prevent unjust detriment.

CASE H: Joe, the sales manager for Company H, promises Sue, a business woman, that she can become a dealer for the widgets manufactured by H if she is approved by H's Board of Directors. Before the Board meets, Joe tells Sue that approval is certain, that the minimum initial order for a dealer is 10,000 units, and that Sue will need warehouse space. Joe even suggests an available building. Sue proceeds to rent a facility and she orders 10,000 units. Thereafter, H's Board fails to approve her as a dealer. If Sue's actions were foreseeable and reasonable, she may be able to recover rental costs and other damages, but she probably will not be able to recover lost profits on the 10,000 units.

In summary on the elements of a contract, who is to do what, by when, must be incorporated into an offer and an acceptance; consideration must be present.

Competitive Bidding

Most commercial contracts are entered into as a result of negotiations, whether limited or extended, between the contracting parties. From time to time, some businesses become involved in alternative mechanisms such as competitive bidding. This method is common for work being done for government agencies and may also occur in private industry. The same basic contract principles apply in the competitive bidding situation; however, the bid documents, in particular the instructions to bidders, become part of the agreement that is accepted by those who respond to the bid. Accordingly, it is particularly important that such instructions be understood and satisfied. Public contracting/competitive bidding and the many unique issues that can arise are a major subset of general contract law and are beyond the scope of this book. Anyone engaging in these activities should become thoroughly familiar with the legal details.

Defaults

Defaults (also called breaches) on contracts occur. This is reality. However, the pursuit of certainty that motivates business people to enter into contracts, legally enforceable promises, is the opportunity for compensation if any damages are sustained. In a sense, by defining obligations, contracts are a form of risk management. (See Chapter 9.) If there is a default and loss, a contract should spell out who bears the risk. Thus, while under a default a promised performance was not fulfilled, the law provides for compensation.

Accepting the fact that defaults will occur, it is important for a manager to monitor performance on a given contract so that potential defaults can be quickly identified. For maximum protection, as soon as a problem is detected the defaulting party should be notified. This step is taken to avoid any contention that the defective performance was known but accepted or waived. Further, **the party who has not defaulted has a legal obligation to minimize or mitigate its damages.** Giving timely notice of a default may permit the defaulting party to deliver replacement goods or provide other substitute performance, thereby minimizing the loss. Further, the sooner the non-defaulting party learns of the default, the quicker it may be able to act to minimize its damages. Such action might include buying substitute goods from other producers or advising its customers of possible resultant delays.

In this regard, business people need to recognize that while the goal of the contract is to have a legally enforceable promise for which damages can be recovered in the event of default, the defaulting party is seldom willing to simply pay over the claimed damages. While there may eventually be a damage recovery, this may entail litigation, including trial and potentially an appeal, all of which takes time. There is also the possibility that there are valid defenses (discussed below) or other factors, such as bankruptcy laws, that may delay or reduce any recovery. Accordingly, as a practical matter, it is best for the non-defaulting party to take an active role in mimizing its damages.

Defenses to Breach of Contract

The law of the land recognizes certain defenses to the performance of obligations under contracts. One defense is **no meeting of the minds** as to essential terms, and, therefore, no contract. Another is a **lack of consideration** as illustrated in Case I.

CASE I: Person X loaned person Y $5,000 to be paid by the following May 25th. On that date, Y approaches X and says she can only pay $4,000. There is no dispute about the full $5,000 being due. Because X needs the money to pay for a car, she accepts and even signs a receipt, prepared by Y, that says "Paid in Full." X would have been better off not signing the receipt as it was worded, but X can still seek repayment of the remaining $1,000 due her because she received no consideration—nothing of value—for signing the receipt that attempted to modify the original contract.

Another defense is **mistake**. If there is a mutual mistake by all the parties involved that is material to the transaction, then there is no contract. The parties are restored to their pre-contract position. If the mistake is unilateral, then as a general rule the contract will be enforceable against the party making the mistake. There are qualifications to this, and courts tend to vary from state to state in their treatment of such matters.

Fraud is sometimes raised as a defense. In its purest sense, *fraud is an intentional misstatement.* However, in many states, even an innocent, but negligent, misrepresentation may make a contract voidable. Further, the fraud or misrepresentation might be by a specific act or by a failure to disclose.

As indicated earlier, the notion of buyer beware is being superseded in most states either by statutory change or by evolutionary change through the common law to a concept of seller beware. Accordingly, even if goods or other property are sold "as is," the seller must disclose known material defects that are not readily discoverable by the purchaser.

A final category of defenses is **impossibility/impracticability**. If one party interferes or prevents performance by the other, then the other is excused. This concept is pretty straightforward. However, if a party's inability to perform is due to other circumstances, then the dispute is more complex. If no one could perform the contract, sometimes referred to as an objective test of impossibility, then performance is excused. On the other hand, if only the particular, obligated party could not perform, referred to as subjective impossibility, then there is no excuse.

A related concept is the Doctrine of Impracticability. This more limited Doctrine might be a defense even though performance is not objectively impossible, provided that the party who is asserting the defense can prove under common law that a) it encountered conditions that were not reasonably foreseeable by the parties when the contract was entered, b) these conditions resulted or would result in the party asserting the defense incurring costs grossly disproportionate to the consideration received, and c) that the party asserting the defense did not assume the risk. The Doctrine of Impracticability is one that is recently adopted by the courts and may vary from jurisdiction to jurisdiction. It is also recognized under the U.C.C.

HOW TO MINIMIZE
YOUR LEGAL TROUBLES

Contracts are entered into to provide a reasonable degree of certainty to people building businesses. Owners, executives, and managers depend on contracts as they make and execute plans. Because contracts are so common and so essential, a given business has a competitive advantage if it is good at contracts. A business person or management team good at contracts will minimize legal troubles for all the parties.

 1. Identify the business objectives to be achieved by a given contract.

In advance of entering into negotiations, determine your specific interest. For example, if you are working on a contract for the sale of goods, are they to meet certain specifications? If so, whose specs? Are the goods to conform to models or samples and, if so, what deviations are permitted? What warranties and representations are required from the seller or, conversely, what warranties or representations will the purchaser permit the seller to disclaim, such as the warranty of merchantability or warranty of fitness for a particular purpose?

 2. Be clear about the details.

Many contract disputes are about the obvious: Who the parties are, the subject matter of the contract, the price or consideration, and the time for performance. The certainty sought via contracts is undercut when these subjects are not clearly and completely spelled out for all to see.

3. Avoid oral contracts for anything vital.

Written documents reduce misunderstanding. While oral contracts can be enforceable, their use should be limited. *No* communication, written or oral, is as precise as it should be, at least from the perspective of an attorney representing a business in a contract dispute. But oral communication adds extra challenges since it is seldom complete and the parties often attach different meanings to the limited words that were used. Then, over time, witnesses disappear, memories falter, and the differences may increase. Except in the simplest of circumstances, it is difficult to justify anything but a written contract.

 4. Read and understand before you sign.

This requirement may seem so obvious that its inclusion here is unnecessary, but **failure to read and understand is a major cause of contract disputes.** Further, most people have a tendency to read what they want the words to say, rather than what they actually say. Many contracts are not simple and they are not easily read and understood, but this does not excuse a business person's failure to take the time to read with care. Defenses to enforcement of a contract based upon ambiguity or failure of the language to state what the parties intended are fairly weak. Occasionally such defenses might succeed, but the probabilities are low. If you don't understand a particular contract term or provision, ask someone who does for an interpretation before you sign.

 5. Monitor contract compliance as you go along. Take action.

The sooner a potential problem is spotted the better. Early warning and prompt action is the best way to keep small issues small. This goes for meeting your own contractual obligations and for insuring that people owing you performance on a promise do what they are suppose to do. Once a small issue heats up into a default, business people usually lose some control over the process and their own destiny in the matter.

6. Use contract amendments sparingly.

Changes may occur during the performance of a contract, and while anything (price, delivery date, specifications, etc.) might be addressed by an amendment to a contract, to become binding any amendment requires the agreement of the other party. Circumstances can change and the other party may refuse to make an amendment or will use it as an opportunity to extract a concession. In addition, except under the U.C.C., an amendment probably must itself be supported by adequate consideration.

7. Use standard forms with care—your own and those of other parties.

Often, in practice, one size does not fit all situations equally well. Significant transactions require well-conceived contracts. Standard forms should not be used for non-standard or complex matters.

CONCLUSION

Contracts are vital tools in building a business. They are, for example, fundamental to risk management in which business risks are addressed and/or passed off to other parties. However, contracts must be used well. Millions upon millions of dollars are wasted by emerging companies each year as a result of broken promises and the ensuing contract disputes that are frequently the direct result of under-managed contract-making processes. Contracts facilitate planning and the execution of plans. Contracts help you make sure you get what you thought you were getting. Without well thought-out and well-defined contracts, business builders have to manage by hope, a difficult task in these competitive times. Contracts and a sound, contract-making process are central to building a business; they deserve the same depth of attention given to the plans for the business they support.

Stay Out of Court and In Business

8

EMPLOYEE HANDBOOKS

"People rise to meet expectations."
-Author unknown

OVERVIEW

Companies are built by people. People work together in different ways. Over the years various managing techniques have each had their turn to be the one best way for accomplishing planned results through people. Managing by objectives, empowerment, and teamwork, to name a few, have all been "the" path at one time or another to quality, customer service, reduced cost or cycle time, sales growth, product development, or some combination. Through it all, however, there has been, and is today, one constant: communication. From employees through supervisors and managers to senior people, everyone favors communication. It transcends all of the other managing techniques, and rightly so. In general, people rise to meet expectations, but to do so they need to know what they are. At the same time, ideas for building a business often come from the people therein, so information needs to flow upwards, organizationally speaking, too. **So communication in a business is a two-way proposition.**

Employee handbooks were initially an attempt at communication. Along with orientation programs, brown-bag lunch chats, managing by walking around, and company newsletters, handbooks were an attempt to provide information. Over the past twenty to thirty years, employee handbooks have become thicker and thicker. Whereas once they summarized benefit programs and the mechanics of vacations and sick leave, for example, today companies often provide a synopsis of company values, policies, and the myriad of federal and state laws that pertain to employees. This is a big task, and the publication of handbooks can involve risks. There are some liabilities associated with this form of communication these days.

In recent years there has been an explosion of law concerning employment. See Chapters 2 and 3. Following in the wake of the law have been claims and lawsuits by employees—past, present, and potential. Employee handbooks as well as written polices and procedures in other communication formats have become a factor in many of the claims and suits. This chapter is about some of the traps inherent in setting forth company policies in employee handbooks and how such handbooks, properly prepared, can work to your benefit.

THE LAW OF THE LAND

The primary issue is quite simple: Is an employee handbook a *contract* between a company and its employees? As explained in Chapter 7, a contract is a legally enforceable promise. In America, we have long had a general "employment-at-will" practice which allows both employers and employees to terminate an employment relationship at any time for any reason, or for no reason at all. (See Chapter 3). In recent years this practice has been eroded by numerous court decisions holding that an employee handbook or policy statement may constitute, under certain circumstances, a *contract* of employment. An employee who has a contract is not an employee "at will."

If a courts finds that a handbook or policy statement is a contract, then an employee making a claim will be entitled to the benefit of the contract, and the employer will be bound to provide it. For example, in a recent court case the employee handbook stated that once a probationary period had been completed, it was the company's policy to discharge employees "for just cause only." The court decision held that this statement created a contract under which the employer could fire an employee only for "just cause." The court noted that the company did not have to publish its human resource policies. It chose to do so for its own interest, and it never told employees that the policies therein would not be applied consistently and uniformly. Thus, even though the parties did not mutually agree to the policy—mutual agreement being a normal prerequisite to the existence of a contract—the company was legally bound to follow it.

Other courts have found limitations to an employer's traditional common-law rights as the result of language in employee handbooks and policy manuals. Here are a few examples:

- An employee handbook setting forth a progressive disciplinary policy was held to be an enforceable contract.
- A managers' manual requiring supervisors to terminate only for cause created an implied contract enforceable by a discharged employee.
- A personnel manual that required supervisors to follow certain procedures before terminating an employee created a contract enforceable by a terminated employee making a claim.

Not all courts, however, have found that employee handbooks contain implied contracts. Decisions vary from state to state. For example, Mississippi courts have repeatedly refused to imply limitations on an employee's at-will status based on an employee handbook. Here the courts have found that a handbook is merely a unilateral statement by an employer and it does not constitute an enforceable contract with employees.

The bottom line is that the content and structure of employee handbooks or other policy statement formats aimed at communication are *very* important to employers. Regardless of the size of a business, a prudent employer is wise to investigate federal, state, and local laws with respect to the applicability of implied contract rules.

This chapter in *Stay Out of Court and In Business* is not an admonition to cease communicating! It *is* aimed at helping you communicate in ways that will not come back to haunt you. A proper handbook can usefully describe expectations and outline policies, programs, and benefits available to eligible employees. It can help set the tone of your organization and convey values that are important in building your enterprise. For smaller and emerging companies unable or unwilling to hire human resource managers and/or staff, handbooks can be a vehicle for providing information in a consistent and interesting way. Such information may be a positive force in helping people succeed in their work and in minimizing friction between management and non-management people.

At the same time, this chapter is not the whole story on employment law, the source of much litigation in these times. A complete coverage of employment law for business owners and managers would require an entire volume of written guidance and multiple days of training. In addition, the contents would vary from state to state.

This chapter *is* intended to highlight pitfalls and offer suggestions in connection with employee handbooks in order to assist you in preventing claims based on such documents.

HANDBOOK CONTENTS

There are three general messages that every employee handbook should convey:

1. In order to protect against your company handbook or policy manual being a contract, you need to expressly state that it merely contains company procedures and is **not a contract**.
2. In order to insure that future changes can be made to the handbook at the will of the employer, you need to expressly include a **reservation of rights** that future revision, supplementation, or rescission of any part can be

made without further notice. Doing so forewarns employees that company procedures can change without their concurrence.

3. In order to reduce the risk of employee lawsuits, your handbook should cover the essence of **major federal, state, and local law** affecting employees and employers. Some of the key areas are: equal employment opportunity, disabilities accommodation, immigration law compliance, employment termination, family leave, drug and alcohol use, and sexual and other unlawful harassment. Sample policies on these subjects are included later in this chapter. Because laws vary from state to state and even within localities in the same state, the sample policies included are illustrative only and must be tailored to your particular situation.

In addition to the subjects above, many employers provide, communicate, information on such topics as:
- Working hours
- Overtime procedures
- Fringe benefits, e.g., vacation and sick leave and the manner in which each is earned
- Medical or other insurance
- Job performance reviews
- Dress code
- Safety procedures or requirements, e.g., equipment needed

In some instances, statements of a company mission or credo, e.g., *The Customer Is Always Right*, are included. As a matter of interest, there are a variety of software programs that business builders can use in developing a comprehensive employee handbook. But the draft should be reviewed carefully, once again, so the finished product does not contain promises, express or implied, and so it is properly tailored to your business. In addition, it is useful to know that a proper employee handbook can actually be an important defense mechanism for a company in connection with issues that sometimes arise with the at-will employees of the enterprise.

HOW TO MINIMIZE YOUR LEGAL TROUBLES

It is useful if the leadership of a business first conscientiously decides whether or not it needs to put its general policies and procedures in writing. Very small business, for example, may choose not to do so. On the other hand, businesses intent on growth, which often involves a lot of people over time, or businesses that operate in multiple physical locations and wish all employees to receive the same message, typically *will* choose to put things in writing. Following are eleven action items with sample wording, where appropriate, to illustrate what can be done in a handbook to minimize legal troubles.

1. Stick to key issues.

Limit your contents to common subjects that are important to the daily interface between employees and their supervisors or managers.

2. Reserve your rights.

Make a clear statement that says the handbook (or whatever

you call it) is not a contract and that it can be changed at any time for any reason without notice.

SAMPLE

<u>Reservation of Rights</u>. This Handbook contains general statements of our policies. It does not constitute, in whole or in part, a contract of employment, nor does it create any contractual rights with regard to your employment.

We must be able to respond flexibly to circumstances as they arise. For this reason, these provisions do not promise specific treatment in specific circumstances. Our policies and practices are subject to change without prior notice. All decisions regarding the application or interpretation of our policies and practices are at our discretion. This applies to all of our policies and practices, whether formal or informal, and whether or not contained in this Handbook, except with regard to our policy against discrimination or harassment. You are entitled to rely on the policies in this Handbook that protect individuals who submit complaints of discrimination or harassment or who cooperate in the investigation of such a complaint. You will be given advance written notice of any change in those complaint policies.

 3. Avoid using absolutes.

Reserve management discretion by staying away from words such as always, never, will, and shall when describing managerial matters. For example, avoid saying you will always follow a specific procedure, e.g., that you will provide counseling sessions in advance of termination when dealing with a situation requiring discipline.

4. Use examples to illustrate general policies.

Employee termination is often a subject included in employee handbooks. Here is a sample of how examples could be used in covering this issue.

SAMPLE

<u>Employment Termination</u>. We may take the corrective action that we deem appropriate. Corrective action may include verbal warnings, written warnings, probation, suspension with or without pay, demotion, reassignment, or discharge. Corrective action may be taken with or without notice or other warning.

The following types of conduct illustrate some of the circumstances for which we may take corrective action:

* Absenteeism or leaving the work site or station without permission;
* Tardiness;
* Alcohol or illegal drug use, or intoxication by alcohol or illegal drug use, while on Company time or while acting as a representative of this Company;
* Theft (including false time records);
* Sloppiness or inattention to work;
* Inappropriate attire;
* Inappropriate or unprofessional behavior;
* Harassing or discriminatory behavior (See Section elsewhere in this Handbook);
* Insubordinate or disrespectful behavior;
* Breaches of confidentiality;
* Conducting personal business on Company time.

We reserve the right in all circumstances to apply the corrective action we determine is appropriate.

We hope that you have a productive and rewarding relationship with us. Nonetheless, employment terminations can occur, and you should understand that your employment with us is "at will." This means that just as you are free to resign at any time, we reserve the right to discharge you at any time, with or without cause or advance notice, and without compensation except for time actually worked, provided the termination is not done for a discriminatory reason in violation of law.

5. Emphasize that your general employees are employed "at will."

In general, do not dilute your relationship with your employees with phrases such as "probationary employee" or "permanent employee." Such wording may create expectations of job security and termination-only-for-cause, or it may imply the existence of employment categories other than "at will."

6. Cover employment discrimination.

The law (see Chapter 3) requires employers not to discriminate against people in certain, protected classes. Here is sample wording that covers three aspects of this issue.

<u>SAMPLE</u>

<u>Equal Employment Opportunity</u>. Our Company is an equal opportunity employer. This means we do not discriminate in employment decisions or policies on the basis of race, color, national origin, creed, religion, sex, age, marital status, physical or mental disability, sexual orientation, or veteran status. This policy applies to all terms and conditions of employment, including hiring, placement, promotion, termi-

nation, reduction in force, recall, transfer, leaves of absence, compensation, and training.

SAMPLE

Disabilities Accommodation. Our Company complies fully with our duty to provide reasonable accommodations to allow people with disabilities to perform the essential functions of their jobs. If you have a disability that limits your ability to perform your job, please let us know so that we can discuss the reasonable accommodations that we may be able to provide.

SAMPLE

Compliance with Immigration Law. Our Company does not discriminate on the basis of ethnicity, national origin, or citizenship status. In accordance with the federal Immigration Reform and Control Act, any offer of employment or continuation of employment is conditioned upon your ability to demonstrate that you are a citizen or a resident alien, or that you have a visa that permits you to work in the United States.

 7. **Cover harassment.**

The law (see Chapter 2) requires companies to provide a non-hostile work experience for their people. Here is sample wording that could be used on this issue.

SAMPLE

<u>Sexual and Other Unlawful Harassment.</u> It is our Company's intent to provide a work environment that is free from all forms of harassment. All employees are expected to be sensitive to and respectful of their coworkers and others with whom they come into contact while representing our Company. We prohibit all of our employees from engaging in any form of harassment, whether due to sex, sexual orientation, race, religion, disability, or any other reason.

With respect to sexual harassment, examples of some of the conduct we prohibit our employees from engaging in include:

- Vulgar or sexual comments, jokes, stories, and innuendoes.
- Graphic or suggestive comments about someone's body or manner of dress.
- Gossip or questions about someone's sexual conduct or orientation.
- Vulgarity, leering, inappropriate touching and obscene or suggestive gestures.
- Display in the work place of sexually suggestive photographs, cartoons, graffiti, and the like.
- Unwelcome and repeated flirtations, requests for dates, and the like.
- Unwelcome sexual advances by a supervisor or a co-worker.
- Solicitation or coercion of sexual activity, dates, or the like by the promise (either express or implied) of rewards or preferential treatment, or by the threat (either express or implied) of punishment.

- Sexual assault.
- Retaliation against an employee for refusing sexual overtures, for complaining about sexual harassment, or for cooperating with the investigation of a complaint.

If at any time you believe you are being subjected to harassment or discrimination, or if you become aware of such conduct being directed at someone else, you should promptly notify_____. If you believe that the person above is involved in the conduct you are concerned about, you should promptly notify_____.

All reported incidents will be investigated under the following guidelines:

- All complaints will be kept confidential, and will be disclosed only as necessary to allow us to investigate and respond to the complaint. No one will be involved in the investigation or response except those with a need to know. Any special concerns about confidentiality will be addressed at the time they are raised.
- Any employee who is found to have violated this policy is subject to corrective action up to and including discharge.
- We will not permit retaliation against anyone who makes a complaint or who cooperates in an investigation.

 8. Describe your general position on drug and alcohol use.

Sample wording for these subjects follows:

<u>SAMPLE</u>

<u>Drug and Alcohol Use</u>. Our employees must be drug free while working for or representing our Company. The possession, use, or trafficking of alcohol or drugs in the work place poses unacceptable risks to the safe, secure, and efficient operation of our business and is strictly prohibited. Employees who are under the influence of alcohol or drugs (whether or not consumed during working hours) while working for or representing us will be subject to corrective action, up to and including discharge. The use, sale, or possession of alcohol or illegal drugs while on Company time or property will also subject the employee to corrective action, up to and including discharge.

 9. Cover family leave if it applies to your business.

The federal Family and Medical Leave Act (FMLA) applies only if an employer meets its jurisdictional limit of 50 employees within 75 miles of where the subject employee works. Some states have laws that overlap with the FMLA and have lower jurisdictional limits or longer periods of leave.

<u>SAMPLE</u>

<u>Family Leave</u>. The FMLA provides up to 12 weeks of unpaid, job-protected leave every twelve months to eligible employees. To be eligible, you must have worked for us at least one year, and for 1,250 hours over the previous twelve months. Unpaid FMLA leave is allowed for the following reasons:
• To care for your child after birth or placement for adoption or foster care.

140

- To care for your spouse, son, daughter, or parent who has a serious health condition.
- For a serious health condition that makes you unable to perform the essential functions of your job.

Accrued paid vacation or sick leave may be substituted for unpaid FMLA leave. We [require] [do not require] that any accrued vacation or sick leave be used in connection with an absence taken under the FMLA.

We require that you provide us with advance leave notice, with medical certification of the need for a leave related to a health condition, and with medical certification of your fitness to return to work after medical leave. Taking leave, or reinstatement after leave, may be denied if these requirements are not met.

If you have any questions about family or medical leave, please contact _____regarding details of the law.

10. Have employees acknowledge receipt of your information.

To increase the chances for effective communication, give employees a specific opportunity to read your handbook or policy descriptions. After they have read the material, ask each of your people to sign a receipt for the handbook or other material, including a notice of at-will employment. At-will employment would not apply to an employee if he or she is a party to a separate, written contract with a specified term of employment.

SAMPLE

EMPLOYEE HANDBOOK RECEIPT. This Employee Handbook describes important information about our Company. By signing below, the undersigned employee understands and acknowledges that:

- The provisions in this Handbook are merely statements of Company policies.
- His or her employment relationship is voluntarily entered into and that there is no set period or length of employment.
- His or her employment can be terminated at will, with or without cause, at any time, so long as there is no violation of applicable law.
- This Handbook is not in whole or in part a contract of employment and nothing contained in this Handbook is intended to create any contractual rights in regard to his or her employement.
- The policies set forth in this Handbook are subject to change from time to time, and, therefore, revisions may be made. Any changes to the Handbook will be communicated through notices to employees. Changes may have the effect of modifying or eliminating existing policies.
- He or she should consult a designated [supervisor, manager, etc.] regarding any questions that he or she may have regarding matters set forth in this Handbook.
- He or she understands that no representative or other employee of the Company has the authority to make any agreements or representations contrary to the provisions of this Handbook.

The undersigned further acknowledges that he or she has received a copy of our Company Employee

Handbook and that it is his or her responsibility to read it and comply with the policies and provisions it contains and in any revisions to the Handbook that may be made in the future.

Signed_____
Name (Print)_____
Date Signed_____

 11. Have employees acknowledge updates of your information.

Any time revisions are made, distribute them to everyone and ask for a signed receipt of the changes. While this may sound like over-kill, it may save you from disputes later on with people who say they didn't get the word.

CONCLUSION

Employee handbooks can be useful tools for communicating certain information to employees. On the other hand, such documents can provide the basis for a claim against an employer if information intended merely as an expression of policy becomes a legally enforceable promise, a contract, with unintended results. Appropriate and conspicuous disclosure of the intention and status of such documents is critical. Properly done, employee handbooks can be a positive force in the building of a business.

Stay Out of Court and In Business

9

RISK MANAGEMENT

"Chance favors the prepared mind."
-Louis Pasteur

OVERVIEW

Being in business entails being at risk. Buildings burn down in the dark of night or are destroyed by an earthquake. Employees become injured even in the presence of five-star safety programs. Machines fail. Contracts to perform are broken. People sue. Most such business risks can be managed to some degree. Buildings and equipment can be insured. People can be trained and insured. Suppliers can be held responsible for their actions, goods, and services. Third parties can agree to pay for certain types of losses if your business experiences them. Managing risks is important because a company crippled by a surprise event or claim is at a competitive disadvantage. Risk Management is about identifying potential surprises and taking away their potential to sting. When you manage risks properly, you get a check in the mail to compensate you after a risk becomes a reality and causes damage. When you leave risks to chance or manage them poorly, you end in court or hurting financially (or both)...or out of business altogether.

There are three common types of risks that business people may seek to manage:

Risks associated with employees
Risks associated with property used in the business
Risks associated with liabilities to third parties

Some risks apply to all businesses; others are inherent within specific industries, e.g., to the airline or pharmaceutical industry.

The most basic tool used to manage risks is a contract which assigns or transfers a specific risk to another party. These are known as **indemnity contracts**. The most common form of indemnity contract is an **insurance** policy. A company (the indemnitee) enters a contract with an insurance company whereby, in return for premiums, it agrees to pay for certain losses sustained by the company. There are other forms of indemnity contracts besides insurance. They are used in private agreements to allocate risk for certain events. This chapter is concerned with both insurance and other methods of allocating risks including the use of indemnity agreements.

Active risk management involves using indemnity contracts to put acceptable boundaries on some economic risks by transferring the risk to others. Active management is also concerned with avoiding taking on risks from others unwittingly.

The following two examples illustrate the allocation of risk through the use of indemnity agreements.

CASE J: *Company J is a designer and manufacturer of hydraulic systems used in aircraft rudder assemblies. Company J's products have for many years been used on numerous types of commercial aircraft. Company B, which manufactures a variety of parts for commercial aircraft, desires to purchase all of the assets of Company J. Company J and Company B enter into a purchase agreement which provides for indemnification as follows: Company J indemnifies Company B against any third-party claims or losses arising out of defective design or manufacture of the hydraulic systems prior to Company B's acquisition of Company J's assets. Correspondingly, Company B indemnifies Company J against any third-party claims or losses arising out of defective design or manufacture of the hydraulic systems after the purchase by Company B of all of Company J's assets and, in essence, the transfer of all operations to Company B.*

Another example of allocating risk through indemnity agreements is shown in Case K.

CASE K: *Company K manufactures custom, high-end computer hardware systems under contract for specific customers. Company K subcontracts the manufacture of many of the components of the hardware systems to other manufacturers. The failure of Company K to receive delivery of given components from a particular subcontractor on time can significantly delay Company K's manufacturing process and ability to deliver to its customers on schedule. Also, Company K warrants to its customers that the systems are free of defect and will function in accordance with agreed specifications. All of Company K's subcontract agreements provide that the subcontractor will indemnify Company K against any claims brought by Company K's customers resulting from defective components supplied by the subcontractor or the failure to deliver the components to Company K on the agreed schedule so that Company K can in turn meet its schedule with its customers.*

THE LAW OF THE LAND

There is very little federal statutory law that pertains to risk management. Most of the law that does exist has been initiated by our states, including the laws that regulate insurance companies. Therefore, each state in which you conduct business will have different requirements pertaining to risk management.

Most states require that all employers except sole proprietors carry individual insurance, workers' compensation insurance as it is called, on their **employees**. Workers' compensation insurance is strictly a creature of statute. Some states create and manage a fund for all employers. Others leave workers' compensation insurance to private insurance companies. The people required to be covered by workers' compensation insurance are defined by statutes. Some employees may elect out and others may be excluded (such as agricultural employees). Workers' compensation insurance does include death benefits.

If **motorized vehicles** are used in a business by its employees, most states require that some minimum level of liability insurance be purchased by the company. Finally, some states are today considering legislation that would require employers to provide general health insurance, a form of risk protection, for employees.

Beyond these coverages and potential coverages for employees, there is little law that requires companies to manage their risks. This means that, for example, most property and business liability insurance is optional.

So, when deciding what to do about managing risk in your business, there are generally three levels of action to consider:

148

1. You can do nothing except buy insurance to meet the minimum legal requirements in the state(s) in which you do business.
2. You can meet your legal minimums and buy additional insurance on selected risks that are beyond those covered by law.
3. You can meet your legal minimums, buy additional insurance on selected risks, and use indemnity agreements to shift other risks to one or more third parties.

These three levels pertain to employees, business property, and business liabilities, the three common types of business risks.

How much risk to actively manage in a particular business is an important, strategic question. It is often addressed in a piecemeal fashion, if at all. This is unfortunate. There are enough essentially *un*manageable risks in most businesses—new products, competitors, technological obsolescence, etc.—that it seems a shame to not mitigate the manageable risks that lend themselves to doing so. In most cases, risk management boils down to an economic decision: Is it worth spending a certain amount of money to protect one's enterprise against the damages that would be sustained *if* something happens that might not happen? The economic analysis techniques are beyond the scope of this book, but the elements of minimizing your legal troubles in connection with risk management follow.

OBJECTS OF COVERAGES

As indicated earlier, there are three major areas of coverage.

Employees

Since workers' compensation insurance is mandatory in most states, this coverage is mainly a matter of determining the requirements and pricing the alternatives offered by various, qualified providers. There is a trend in recent years toward employers using **temporary employees** or subcontractors rather than permanent employees to perform work. One of the reasons for doing this is to avoid the costs of workers' compensation insurance. However, this is an increasingly risky proposition as both states and the Internal Revenue Service are aggressively challenging the use of temporary workers in certain circumstances.

For example: Company A has an employee stock option plan for all of its regular employees. Company A has for years regularly employed temporary employees and "independent contractors." If truly temporary or independent, these individuals would not be qualified to participate in the stock option plan. However, continuous use of temporary employees or independent contractors over an extended period of time could result in their being deemed regular employees by the state or the IRS. Such an unanticipated designation or result would obviously have a significant impact on the company and its employee stock option plan.

The requirements and documentation associated with classifying a temporary employee or an independent contractor as such seem to be escalating. For example, the IRS has a procedure which examines twenty issues to determine whether or not someone is an employee or an independent contractor. If "temps" or "subs" are found to really be "employees" by the government and/or the courts, **employers face stiff tax and liability costs,** including those associated with lawsuits for the cost of injuries sustained by those so employed by the enterprise.

> *CASE L: Company L, which designs and manufactures custom software systems enters into a consulting agreement with an expert in the field who will assist in designing a new system. Under the terms of the consulting agreement, the consultant is deemed to be an independent contractor (even though his or her benefits and duties are similar to those of a regular employee) and, as such, the consultant is responsible for payment of his or her own income taxes on the income generated through the contract. The contract continues for a period of one year during which Company L does not, as it would in regard to regular employees, withhold any taxes from the payments to the consultant. On audit, the IRS later determines that the consultant is in fact an employee and not an independent contractor and, unfortunately, the consultant never paid his or her own income taxes. Company L ends up having to pay the additional taxes that it should have withheld from the payments to the consultant.*

One other form of employee insurance that companies, particularly growing companies, should consider is **key man** insurance which is a form of life and/or disability insurance with benefits payable to the company. Often the success of growing companies relies heavily on one or more vital individuals. The loss of any one of them would be a setback to the company and retard its rate of growth. Many companies, therefore, purchase key man insurance on such individuals to insure against the risk that they might die or become disabled. The insurance money would compensate the company for such loss and help pay the cost of replacing the person.

Property

Most operating companies make products or provide services that depend on buildings, equipment, inventory, software, and various tangible assets used by employees. The complete loss of the use of physical assets can be catastrophic. The partial loss of use can also be costly, e.g., you can lose momentum in the marketplace because you are out of operation for a period of time.

There are four ways to manage the risks associated with your company property:

• **Purchase insurance** to cover the loss of a particular asset used in the business. Most businesses, for example, have fire insurance. Many manufacturing businesses have inventory insurance. Some businesses have insurance on their computers and/or software. A more exotic example of insuring a physical asset would include livestock used in breeding. Other examples of unique insurance would include special events insurance, i.e., a promoter of a concert might purchase insurance to cover his or her costs in the event the performing artist cancels the concert.

• **Negotiate indemnity agreements** with outside, third parties. Again, an example of these kinds of indemnity agreements would be those that a manufacturer has with its suppliers or subcontractors.

   For example, if your company leases computers to customers, the leasing agreement you use can specifically provide that the renter will pay for any damage to the equipment while it is in the renter's possession. Then, if your equipment is lost or damaged while on lease, you are protected against the loss. You have managed that risk.

For another example, you could pay me [B] to agree to indemnify, defend and hold you [A] harmless from and against any and all claims, demands, liabilities, losses, costs, damages, attorney fees, and expenses of whatever kind or nature which may arise by reason of, or in consequence of [identify the activity here], including but not limited to sums paid for settlement of claims, and expenses, including attorney fees, incurred in connection with enforcing the terms of our specific agreement.

• **Self insure**. Some companies, particularly very large companies, elect to self-insure certain risks because, based upon their internal risk management analysis, they are economically in a position to do so and it is economically smart for them to do so. Also, many companies end up self-insuring a portion of their risk by virtue of the deductibles on their insurance policies.

• **Develop redundancies** in your company so that the loss of a single, key property does not cripple the entire enterprise. For example, products can be made and inventoried at more than one location; backup copies of software and customer information can be stored in underground vaults; and two vendors can be chosen and used for critical parts. At first glance some of the above steps may seem extreme. Chances are most would not be taken *just* to manage the risk of loss. But risk reduction might tip the scales in favor of, say, multiple plant sites in a strategic decision on the matter. For example, most of the semiconductor manufacturers which started in Silicon Valley atop the famous San Andreas (earthquake) fault line now have plants outside the area, no doubt for a variety of reasons. But risk management is most likely one of them.

Company Acts & General Liability

Corporations, under the law, have "limited" liability, but they still have it. This means they can be held financially responsible for accidents, malpractice (in the case of professional corporations), chemical spills (environmental liability), and so on.

In some fields such as contracting and businesses requiring state licenses, liability insurance may be required by law. Most companies purchase liability insurance to cover their general exposure. Some companies also purchase liability insurance to cover industry-specific exposure such as companies manufacturing toxic materials. A few companies, e.g., chemical companies, drug manufacturers, chain saw manufacturers, gun manufacturers, and nuclear power plants, self-insure all or a portion of their exposures because of the high risk and/or high cost involved. Sometimes risks are essentially uninsurable, e.g., those associated with nuclear radioactive products, including disposal.

HOW TO MINIMIZE YOUR LEGAL TROUBLES

Most legal troubles in the area of risk management stem from one of two sources. A company either fails to comply or acts in an illegal manner with regard to state regulations, or it ends up in a contract dispute with a third party regarding an insurance policy or other type of indemnification agreement. Below are six actions business leaders can take to consciously deal with the risk profiles of their enterprises.

1. Identify risks inherent to the business.

Besides the generic risks mentioned above, farmers and touring companies face weather risks, food companies have contamination risks, and banks must contend with robberies. Not all risks are insurable, and sometimes the premiums are too high to insure a given risk. Other risks, however, lend themselves to very creative approaches to mitigation. A systematic review of a business in its totality with an eye toward risk management is the best first step toward minimizing legal troubles in this area. A prudent management team will examine the balance sheet of its company, find out what is rented, leased, borrowed, or otherwise contracted for that is not on the balance sheet, and isolate special, potential sources of economic exposure that are peculiar to the work of the enterprises. For example, companies that transport bulk oil in transport ships must consider the economic risks associated with a spill. A legal audit (see Chapter 10) can be helpful in this identification and evaluation process.

Rank in order of priority the risks of the business you may wish to manage starting with the ones you are required to cover, like workers' compensation, and running through such ultimate issues as the death of a key personality to total business interruption.

 2. Use industry-knowledgeable help to evaluate alternatives.

Most managers are wise to use the help of specialists when negotiating cost-effective commercial insurance policies and indemnity agreements. While workers' compensation insurance is usually relatively straightforward and competitively priced, often due to state legislation and regulations of state insurance commissioners, other risk management instruments vary greatly in cost and coverage details. Aggressive shopping is required.

For example, fire and property damage insurance policies can cover actual cost or replacement cost. They can cover "all risks" (including damage or collapse due to design or construction defects) or just basic fire and storm damage. Insurance for such things as earthquake or flood damage would not normally be covered, even under an all-risk policy, without special endorsement.

A blanket liability policy may include product liability protection (see Chapter 5), coverage for employment discrimination suits (see Chapter 3), and protection for the negligence of others. A stripped down policy may cover only basic liability such as liability for your own negligent acts.

 3. Use indemnity agreements where appropriate.

As discussed above, indemnity agreements or provisions should be used where there is an identifiable risk and that risk can properly be transferred to another party. As examples, indemnity provisions should typically be used in the following kinds of transactions or agreements:

- Purchase Agreements in regard to the purchase and sale of businesses. These agreements would typically include indemnity provisions allocating the risk for past and future liabilities between the former and new owner of the business.
- Subcontract Agreements. Where manufacturers or contractors use the services of others or incorporate products supplied or manufactured by others into their own products, indemnity provisions would typically be used to allocate the risk of third-party claims made by users or consumers arising from defect or malfunction.
- Agreements between manufacturers and designers. These kinds of agreements would typically contain indemnity provisions allocating the risk of liability for third party claims between the design component and the manufacturing component.

The bottom line is that nearly every significant business transaction involves an issue of risk allocation. The prudent business manager should not overlook the opportunity to allocate risks to others where appropriate.

4. Be careful what you sign!

Many everyday business agreements such as purchase orders, rental contracts, leases, and service contracts include indemnity provisions. This means that when you sign something you may assume someone else's risk unknowingly. They pass off their risk to you! Many busy managers and executives—too many, really—scoff at the "boilerplate" language that often accompanies everyday business agreements. **Scoff at your peril**. When things go bad, you may find yourself on the hook.

An example of a seemingly innocuous document is the typical car rental agreement which obligates you to pay for any damage done to the vehicle regardless of whether it was your fault or the total cost involved. You become the strict insurer of that vehicle while it is in your possession, even in cases where the vehicle may be defective, resulting in an accident and damage to the vehicle. It's not your car, but you end with a bill to pay. Similar provisions show up in a variety of standard, everyday business agreements.

In taking care of what you sign, you may *knowingly* undertake liability for someone else's risk because doing so is to your advantage. And you may be able to purchase insurance to cover your potential costs if you end up with a claim.

5. Submit precise claims quickly.

When a loss occurs and you believe you are covered by an insurance policy or an indemnity agreement, submit your claim with all the details immediately to your insurance company, broker, or the third party involved. Promptness and completeness is important because it reduces the chances of intervening events muddying the issues or evidence involved in the claim.

For example, suppose Company A has a claim against it but fails to notify its insurance carrier. Then suppose A defends itself against the claim but loses and has a judgment entered against it. Company A *then* notifies its carrier. The insurance carrier would likely claim breach of policy, prejudice, and no coverage due to the delayed notification.

Once an insurance company or a third party receives a claim, it will usually conduct an investigation to determine whether the claimed loss or potential loss falls within the policy or agreement. Such an investigation may provide you with valuable information at little or no cost. For example, the investigation may reveal a safety problem unknown up to that point. The investigating company will tell you, the insured, whether it agrees that the loss or potential loss is covered. At this point the clarity of the underlying policy or indemnity agreement involved becomes critical.

It is not unusual for a claim to involve three parties: An employee, customer, or vendor; your company; and an insurance provider. For example a customer might sue your company because he or she claims a product of yours is defective. In a case such as this, your insurance company will likely investigate your claim to them and decide whether or not it will defend you in the lawsuit. A timely, documented claim by you will be helpful to your company in both garnering the active support of your carrier and in any court action resulting from the claim.

Today insurance companies are becoming especially vigilant in their search for fraudulent claims. Documentation is your best offense—and your best defense. For example, if you have a fire loss in your business, prior to submitting your claim you should document in detail the value of all the important items destroyed in the fire. In addition to your accounting records and perhaps a photographic record, your own legal audit (covered in Chapter 10) can help you provide substance to your claim. Also note: If an insurance company ever asks to take a statement from you under oath, do so only after obtaining professional advice on the matter.

 6. Stay Current.

Businesses evolve. Products are introduced and dropped. Offices are opened and closed. Political agendas thrive and dive. People come and go. Risks ebb and flow. To manage risks you have to know what they actually are in a given business right now, today; not what they used to be or what you wish they were, but what they really are. **Reality**. Most companies have annual budgets that reflect hopes for the days ahead. Many companies have strategic plans for the longer term. Risk management deserves a place on the agenda in any serious discussion about building a company for the long haul.

CONCLUSION

Risk management, at the extreme, can be quite complex. As outlined above, nearly every business transaction of consequence involves an issue of risk allocation. Proactive risk management can minimize the legal troubles that arise from neglect or lack of foresight when it comes to protecting a company's assets against unwanted surprises.

10

CHOOSING & USING AN ATTORNEY

"If there were no bad people, there would be no good lawyers."

-Charles Dickens (1812-1870)

OVERVIEW

Business dominates center stage of our society these days. A recent survey published by a consortium of two dozen universities and research groups found that "37% of the 100 million U.S. households include someone who has founded, tried to start, or helped fund a small business." Americans start over 200,000 new businesses a year according to Dun & Bradstreet's commercial credit database. Entrepreneurs are our national heroes and heroines. And corporate chieftains now enjoy wealth and rank that make the kings and queens of old pale in comparison. Is it any wonder, then, that businesses have become the focal point of change in all its dimensions? A famous bank robber once said during an interview in his jail cell that he robbed banks "because that's where the money is." Today, everyone with a cause looks first at businesses for relief, for businesses are where the money is.

The primary mechanism for relief is the law of the land. As indicated in Chapter 1, it comes from three sources: statutes which are created by legislation enacted by state and federal elected officials; common law which is created by judges as they deal with specific cases that come to their court rooms; and regulations generated by government agencies such as the EPA—Environmental Protection Agency. In recent years, there has been an explosion of new law from these three sources, particularly from regulations. Much of it affects the operation of companies. Therefore, law is, or should be, of more than a peripheral interest to people in business.

Historically, business people have relied on attorneys to handle occasional legal matters or problems. Today, at center stage, it is difficult to keep legal questions occasional. As a practical matter, business people have two or three choices. One, they can try to keep up on the law themselves. Two, they can hire help. Or, three, some few can opt to step out of the spotlight and pursue another calling.

To respond to choice two, there are today almost **700,000 lawyers** in the United States, about one per every 100 working people in the country. This is the highest ratio of attorneys per capita on earth. By comparision, there are fewer than 15,000 lawyers in Japan, but this raw number is somewhat misleading. In the words of Ewell E. Murphy, a partner in the Houston firm of Baker & Botts: "Lawyers in the United States do things which need doing, but in other countries those things are done mostly by non-lawyers or by accountants, executives, bureaucrats, commissars, Zen abbots, witch doctors, Mafia capos, fakirs, country squires, feather merchants, and other assorted movers and shakers."

Some 150,000 of the 700,000 attorneys in the United States are staff attorneys employed by roughly 6,500 corporations. These same corporations engage independent outside counsel to the tune of approximately $7 billion each year. Most of it is spent with the 1,200 largest law firms which, in the aggregate, employ some 60,000 attorneys. In total, then, at least 200,000 of the attorneys in our land are primarily engaged in legal matters revolving around companies. The remainder concentrate on legal work concerning individual matters.

BUILDING A BUSINESS

Most businesses are built with team effort. While one or two key people often set the pace in the early going, the complexities, including legal considerations, make it difficult for founders to develop companies of any size without a team composed of individuals with multiple talents. There are two rings of members. First, the inside ring usually consists of people with strengths in the various functions required by a particular business—sales, science, accounting, manufacturing, etc. It is vital that this inside ring be made up of qualified people who can work hard together, day-by-day, towards agreed upon, shared objectives.

The second, outside ring, consists of advisors who bring specialized know-how to the enterprise, often on an as-needed basis. Directors, CPAs, attorneys, insurance brokers, technical specialists, advertising people, and bankers are candidates for this outer ring. **People in the outside ring need to be selected with the same care**

as those on the inside one. To the extent that they are, the chances of the business succeeding are improved. But too often, members of the outside ring are chosen casually or as a matter of convenience such as when an attorney or CPA is selected to work on business matters on the basis of what she or he did or does on personal matters. Attorneys, at least, should be chosen on the basis of their proven credentials for helping build a business.

LAW OF THE LAND

Attorneys are licensed to practice state by state. This is consistent with the fact that so much law that affects businesses is created at the state level. An attorney must pass a state bar exam before he or she can practice in a given state. It is important to note that attorneys are subject to ethics and conflicts of interest rules adopted by state bar associations. Attorneys are also generally subject to consumer protection laws (see Chapter 6) on the same basis as other service providers.

CHOOSING AN ATTORNEY

Good business attorneys are not household names! Such attorneys are adept at keeping their clients' problems and their own names out of the press. A famous attorney is probably *in*appropriate for your business! So how do you find the right legal resource for your outside ring? There are four subjects involved:

Identifying the legal requirements of your business.
Finding qualified candidates.
Deciding which individual or firm to engage.
Estimating costs.

Legal Requirements of Your Business

What are your likely legal needs? Is yours a highly technical company with many intellectual property questions? A high-growth business with ambitions to sell an IPO (Initial Public Offering) of stock in a few years? An international company with more and more contracts in China or South Africa? A retailer with stores in several states and suppliers in Europe? A manufacturer with plans for a continuing series of new products? A franchise restaurant owner? The possibilities are endless! And each scenario suggests somewhat different legal fronts with which you, ideally, ought to be familiar if you are to indeed minimize your legal troubles. In selecting an attorney, **the preferred candidate is one who has traveled the road you are planning to travel.** It is not always the case that an individual attorney or firm will have exactly the precise experience you (will) require, but the trick is to get as close to it as you can. Otherwise, you will be paying with your quarters for him, her, or them to learn!

This approach is dependent upon your having some idea of where you are going. Perhaps you operate with something less grand than a strategic plan, but most builders of businesses have at least a direction in mind. And most can look to one or two companies similar to their own (but a little bigger) as role models. Use such a role model to predict what sort of legal issues you can expect to encounter in the years ahead, and then seek a legal partner for your team who individually, or together with others in a firm, has direct experience with the issues you have identified. This process is no different than selecting a physician. If you have a family history of heart disease, you will probably want to have a personal physician who has at least some strong credentials in the subject.

Finding Qualified Candidates

Attorneys differ. With your specifications in hand, ask people whose opinion you respect for recommendations of attorneys with qualifications that meet your needs. A short list of sources would include venture capitalists, CPAs, bankers, particularly investment bankers, management people in related businesses, and, perhaps, personal friends who are attorneys but non-candidates for one reason or another. It is also possible to consult the Martindale-Hubbell law directory, the only comprehensive directory of lawyers. It can be found at your local library. This directory lists most attorneys and rates many of them on the basis of their experience and reputation among other attorneys. Though the Martindale system is far from perfect, it provides an assessment based on frequent mailings to people in the profession as well as interviews of lawyers and judges.

Once you have identified candidates—individuals or firms—it is important to vigorously interview them, just as you would any other key player for your team. In addition to reviewing qualifications, interviews provide an opportunity for a personal "chemistry check." Sooner or later an attorney who is a full member of a business's outside ring gets to know the most intimate details of an enterprise—hirings, firings, contracts, insurance policies, employee claims, patents, etc. It is important to have in such a role someone (or a firm) with whom you are comfortable. Your comfort should not be based on compliance or subservience, however. **An attorney who will tell you exactly what you want to hear doesn't add much value to your business.** You need someone qualified and willing to tell you what you need to hear with regard to the law of the land and how it is practiced. The right attorney or firm will work hard to keep you out of court and in business.

Individual Attorneys vs. Firms

The chapter headings of this book provide a handy reference list of the areas in which most companies encounter legal questions as they grow. **No one attorney can master the evolving intricacies of all such areas of the law.** But one individual can know enough to know when to bring in specialists. So, it is possible to hire an individual as your primary advisor on legal matters if you can find one who meets your needs and has ready access to others in the profession.

A legal firm is typically made up of specialists in a variety of legal subjects who together are able to provide "full service" to their clients. A firm should have (and pass along some of the benefits of) certain efficiencies that a collection of individuals might not have. This is particularly true as more and more legal work has a computer component to it. Also, a firm should provide for continuity and an easy transition from one attorney to another over time as individuals age, new specialties are added, new services are needed, and so forth. Typically, the attorney you choose acts as a "point man" handling many of your legal needs while at the same time bringing in others when they are deemed necessary and appropriate.

Costs

The good news on fees is that the legal industry is much more competitive than it used to be. Today most individual attorneys and law firms are used to bidding for corporate business. A qualified person or firm understands budgets and cost/benefit analysis. The bad news is that sound legal work requires the use of highly trained and experienced people, and such people cost money. However, properly used (see below), your investment in attorneys should give you a satisfactory rate of return. When choosing between qualified candidates to be on your team, ask them what the fees will be and how they will be calculated. However, bear in mind that although cost *is* a factor, it is not likely to vary significantly between attorneys with similar qualifications, and ultimately the cost may be a minor and worthwhile factor in building your business.

One word of caution: **Avoid, in most circumstances, giving your attorney stock in your company in lieu of cash for services rendered.** It is tempting, particularly in emerging companies, for management to pay for services with shares to conserve much-needed cash. But doing so can lead to tainted legal advice. You want and need an attorney who will provide dispassionate advice, not as a shareholder, but as a truly independent counselor. In addition, from time to time you may need to put an attorney off of your team for any one of a number of reasons. It is more difficult to do so when that person is also a shareholder.

In summary, choosing an attorney is an important event. She or he or the firm should have the capacity to be a key player in building your business over the long haul. An attorney should be viewed as a member of your team. And once you choose an attorney, you need to use her or him well.

USING AN ATTORNEY

Managing is a process of achieving planned results through others. The planned results you want from your attorney will vary over the life of your enterprise. In general, the action items below are designed to maximize the return you get on the investment you most probably have to make to use the law to your competitive advantage.

1. Aim to prevent legal troubles.

Attorneys are best used prophylactically. It is far better to have her or him read a contract, lease, advertisement, or an employee handbook before you approve and use it than afterwards when problems arise. After the fact, you and your company are on the defense. Before the fact, you are still on offense.

2. Treat your attorney as a full member of your team.

Invite him or her to attend key meetings and other formative events so he or she can understand what is going on in the life of the enterprise. You want your attorney to know the intricacies of your business. Then he or she will know enough to raise questions (and suggest answers) sooner rather than later. He or she might even spot opportunities that can work to your company's advantage. For example, your attorney might help you better minimize your risks in a business transaction or structure a deal to maximize tax benefits. At a minimum, he or she can often serve as a neutral sounding board or reality checker, as someone not caught up in the emotion of the products, markets, and technologies of the moment.

3. Ask your attorney to identify any legal issues that might arise from changes in your business strategy.

Do you plan to introduce some radically new products? What about patents, copyrights, product liabilities, warranties, etc? Are you expecting to move aggressively into new market segments, e.g., new states or distribution channels? What fresh issues await you, and what will they cost to mitigate? For example, each state has its own franchise law. Your plans may unknowingly place your company within the legal definition of franchising somewhere. Surprise! In many places there are harsh penalties for being an unwitting franchiser who has not followed the local legal requirements.

 4. Do a legal audit periodically as you change in size and complexity.

As you add/subtract employees, facilities, locations, and vendors, including bankers, it pays to review protective devices such as insurance policies, indemnity agreements, loan papers, employee handbooks, even the content of orientation programs for new people. Like an annual physical for your key people, a systematic, high-quality review of the administrative side of your business is important and can be productive in preventing problems later on. A legal audit on various aspects of your business from time to time can proactively reduce risks and save money. A sample legal audit is included at the end of this book.

 5. Rely on your attorney for guidance on corporate governance.

There are a lot of mechanical "to dos" to keep a corporation healthy in the sight of various state and federal agencies. Board meetings need to be held; resolutions need to be passed; minutes need to be kept; stock purchase agreements need to be in order; and regulatory filings need to be made. And the requirements escalate dramatically if you are a company selling securities or seeking to raise capital. For example, most states have very restrictive "Blue Sky" laws for protecting their citizens from investment schemes. If you raise money improperly and run afoul of such a law, you can damage your company's prospects for public financing for years to come and be subject to sanctions, penalties, and civil liabilities.

 6. Create approved forms and procedures for repetitive events with legal overtones.

Purchase-order terms, for example, can be codified, approved by your attorney, and used repeatedly throughout your organization. The same is true of other routine documents. Have your attorney do them right, once, and then review them periodically as part of his or her legal audit.

 7. Ask your attorney to keep your managers and supervisors up to date on key subjects with legal ramifications.

For example, depending on the nature of your business and its products/services, you and your people need to be kept up to date on any changes in the relevant law. Periodic training and refresher sessions go a long way to minimizing problems.

 8. Insist on a thorough, cost/benefit analysis of any major legal initiatives or responses to claims.

Strive to take the emotion out of litigation, or threats of litigation. As suggested in the first chapter, *The Last Resort: Court*, litigation is a fact of life and it is best treated as a *business* issue, not a moral one. It is impossible to over-estimate the stress that accompanies litigation, whether you win or lose. It should be approached with great care and clear heads.

9. Go easy on the attorney jokes.

Everyone has them, even attorneys! But their use within an organization by people in leadership roles undercuts respect for the law and may cause people to wink at it as they conduct the affairs of your enterprise. The language of a clan, such as the people who make up a company, has a big impact on the culture of that clan. In fact, language is a major determinant of a culture. And a culture drives behavior. If you trust an attorney to be part of your team, it is wise to respect her or his profession and advice. If you do *not* trust your attorney, find a replacement that you do!

10. Conduct periodic performance reviews of your attorney.

Chances are good that from time to time you look hard at most of the advisors who make up the outside ring of your team, e.g., your CPA, advertising agency executive, insurance broker, banker, etc. Look hard at your attorney too. He or she needs to know both your expectations and level of satisfaction. In general, qualified, professional people tend to rise to meet expectations, if they know them.

11. Conduct regular evaluations of your business's legal needs.

It is important to determine whether your legal representation is adequate for your business's changing needs. Does your current attorney have the experience to handle any new legal issues that you are likely to face, in light of your plans? Even if your attorney is performing well, is it time to add incremental legal expertise in your outer ring?

CONCLUSION

Many companies grow to the point where they have their own, in-house legal staff. Along the way they rely on outside, independent counsel. In either case, the business is best served if the attorneys involved are well chosen and used purposefully. The law applicable to business unfolds daily; in many respects it is a moving target. This being so, an attorney integrated in the life of a company is better able to minimize legal troubles *for that company* than one who is only casually acquainted with the business. And minimizing legal troubles is the purpose of this book. An attorney who is truly on your team is in the best position to prevent many problems and respond objectively with precise advice to those that do arise. Attorneys are an investment. Your rate of return is a function of how well they are used.

CONDUCTING A LEGAL AUDIT

Properly conducted, a legal audit is a practical way to stay atop your legal affairs and, thereby, help you minimize legal troubles for your business. Basically, a legal audit is like a physical exam you get from your physician. You try to ascertain your current condition, correct any problems, and take action to prevent future problems.

A legal audit can be broad or narrow, depending on the nature of the business and the stakes involved. For example, a broad audit could include a look at operations to insure compliance with occupational safety and environmental regulations. A narrow audit could be limited to a simple review of corporate records and licenses. Many advocates of legal audits start with a look at the operating statements, financial audits, and business plans of a particular company.

Following is a comprehensive checklist that covers the basic areas that would normally be included in a legal audit. This checklist can stand on its own; it can also serve as a starting point for those wishing to develop a custom checklist for a particular business.

LEGAL AUDIT CHECKLIST

Status/Review of Licenses, Registrations, etc.

____ Is the company's state license current?

____ Is the company properly registered in every state or jurisdiction in which it conducts business?

____ Is the information on file (address, directors, officers, agents, etc.) with state and other jurisdictions current?

____ Have all required, periodic filings with government agencies been taken care of on schedule?

____ Is there a calendar/schedule for the company's periodic or future filings?

Status/Review of Minutes and Resolutions

____ Are company minutes and resolutions from board meetings current and in sufficient detail to reflect actions taken and decisions made?

____ Are stock and shareholder records current?

____ Are tax matters being properly reviewed and handled?

Status/Review of Significant Contracts, Leases, etc.

____ Have all significant business transactions and agreements that have been entered into been properly put into writing?

____ Are there any contracts, leases, or other agreements where the company is concerned about the other party's ability to perform?

____ Are there any contracts, leases, or other agreements where the company is concerned about its ability to perform on its obligations?

____ Are there any contracts, leases, or other agreements that the company may wish to terminate?

____ Are there any contracts, leases, or other agreements which the company may wish to amend?

____ Are there any contracts, leases, or other agreements which the company may wish to renew? Or redo in the form of a new document?

Review/Update Standard Documents, Invoices, etc. (Forms)

____ Are the company's existing, standard forms consistent with applicable laws?

____ Are the company's existing, standard forms consistent with its current operations. For example, has the company added new product lines or services, or has it expanded into new, geographical areas or channels of distribution which would dictate different forms or terms?

____ Has the company run into any problems with its use of its standard forms?

____ Do existing forms give the company every possible advantage that it could have? For example, do they include provisions for attorneys fees in case of a dispute? Do they provide for interest payments? Do they include appropriate indemnification provisions?

Status/Review of Insurance Coverage & Indemnity Agreements

____ Does the company have pending insurance claims?

____ Are insurance coverages adequate for current operations?

____ Has the company considered coverage for evolving areas of law where it might have exposure, e.g., employment law?

____ Has the company entered into any agreements involving indemnification or other significant risk allocation arrangements that may suggest additional or different insurance coverage?

Status/Review of Employee Issues, Employment Contracts, and Employee Handbooks

____ Are employee handbooks current with applicable law and company policy?

____ Have there been any employee claims that indicate the need for a different policy or enforcement procedure than now exists?

____ Are there any employment contracts with key people that should be reviewed, or which may be coming up for renewal?

____ Has the company hired any key people who are not a party to a written employment contract with the company?

____ Are all key employees, including those with technical knowledge or expertise and those who have access to company trade secrets and confidential information, subject to adequate nondisclosure and noncompetition agreements with the company?

Status/Review of Stock Options and Stock Option Plans

____ Has the company granted any stock options to key employees, and, if so, have they been properly documented?

____ Are the records of any Stock Option Plan current?

____ Have any stock options been exercised, and, if so, are the transactions properly recorded?

Status/Review of Pending Litigation, Including Contingent or Threatened Claims

____ Are there any claims or potential claims that should be addressed before litigation begins?

____ Should insurance carriers be notified of any current or pending claims?

____ Are there any claims or potential claims that could directly effect or limit the company's operations, e.g., claims by customers, competitors, or suppliers?

Other Review Items

____ Is the company taking full advantage of copyright, patent, and registration possibilities?

____ Is the company taking adequate action to identify and protect its trade secrets and confidential information?

____ Are there any significant changes or proposed changes in the laws applicable to the company's operations that might affect operations or planning in the future?

____ Is the company conducting employee training on important matters such as workplace sexual harassment, employment discrimination, product liability, unfair business and trade practices, etc.?

KEY WORD GLOSSARY

Antitrust Laws: Statutes designed to protect trade and commerce from unlawful restraints and to promote free competition in the marketplace.

Attorney in Fact: Person authorized to act as a legal agent or representative of another.

Attorney at Law: Person authorized by a state's highest court or by a federal court to prosecute and defend actions in that jurisdiction; a person licensed by a state bar association to provide legal services.

Breach: A party's failure to perform an agreed-upon or contracted obligation; failure to comply with a legal duty to another; a default.

Common Law: The body of law created by the courts. The common law is based upon custom and judicial precedent rather than written or statutory law.

Complaint: The document filed with a court that sets forth a plaintiff's claims and commences legal action.

Consideration: Something of value given in exchange for the performance or promise of performance by another. Often described as "the inducement to a contract," consideration is generally required for an agreement between parties to be binding as a contract.

Contract: A legally enforceable promise or agreement between parties.

Damages: Monetary compensation awarded by law to one who has suffered loss or injury due to the actions of another.

Defendant: Person or company against whom a claim is made in a legal action; the party who responds to a plaintiff complaint.

Indemnity: Obligation or duty to secure against present or future losses incurred by another acting at his or her request or for his or her benefit.

Injunction: Judicial remedy, most often in the form of an order or judgement, requiring one to do or stop doing something.

Liability: Obligation to do or not do something; often a duty to pay money. Also refers to one's responsibility for his or her conduct.

Litigation: Court contest between at least two parties.

Plaintiff: Person or company who initiates legal action throught the filing of a complaint.

Proprietary: Owned by a particular entity.

Quid Pro Quo: One thing for another. When used in legal contexts, synonymous with consideration.

Regulations: Rules with the effect of law which are created by a government agency.

Remedy: Legal means or basis to recover a right or redress a wrong; the legal redress granted by a court.

Statute: Law created by a legislative body.

Tort: A wrong or injury resulting from a breach of a legal duty which does not exist by virtue of a contract or private realtionship.

Warranty: An assurance by one party to a contract of a fact regarding the subject of a contract, upon which the other party may rely.

INDEX

Audits. *See* Legal audits
Authors. *See* Copyrights
Automobile insurance, 148

B

Bench trials, 20
Bidding, competitive, 118
Binding arbitration, 24-25
Boilerplate language, 157
Breach of contract, 17, 119-120
  defenses to, 120-121
  defined, 182
  impossibility/impractibility of
  performance, 121
  minimizing legal problems, 122-124
Breach of warranty, 17
  by product seller, 83-84
Building businesses, 163-164

C

Car rental agreements, 157
Caveat emptor, 107
Cease and desist orders, 95
Certainty requirements for contracts,
115
Champion, S. G., 109
Civil Rights Act of 1964. *See* Title VII
  of Civil Rights Act of 1964
Civil Rights Act of 1991, 29-30
Clayton Act, 98
Common law, 19
  copyright protection, 68
  defined, 181
  employee handbooks and, 130
  trademark protection, 64
Competitive bidding, 118
Complaints, 19-20

Confidential information. *See* Trade
secrets
Conflicts of interest, 164
Consideration for contracts, 116-118
  defined, 182
  lack of consideration defense to
  breach, 120
Construction defects, liability for, 86
Consumer protection. *See
also* Product liability
  laws pertaining to, 94-97
  minimizing legal problems, 105-106
  types of claims, 99
Contracts, 109-125. *See also* Breach
of contract; Consideration for
contracts; Indemnity contracts
  acceptance as element of, 112-116
  amendments to, 124
  bidding, competitive, 118
  certainty requirements, 115
  clarity of, 122
  collateral agreements, 116
  counteroffers, 112
  defined, 109, 182
  elements of, 111-118
  employee handbooks as, 129-130
  exchange of promises, 114
  extrinsic evidence of, 115-116
  laws pertaining to, 110-111
  minimizing legal problems, 122-124
  offer as element of, 112-116
  oral contracts, 114, 122
  output contracts, 117
  parole evidence rule and, 115-116

(EPA), 162
Equal Employment Opportunity
Commission (EEOC). *See* EEOC
(Equal Employment Opportunity
Commission)
Ethics, 164
Express warranty, 84
Extrinsic evidence of contracts, 115-
116

F

Family and Medical Leave Act
(FMLA), 140-141
Family leave policy, 140-141
Federal courts, 19
Federal Trade Commission (FTC). *See*
FTC (Federal Trade Commission)
Fees. *See* Attorneys' fees
Fire insurance policies, 155-156
Flood insurance, 156
Foreign countries
  patent protection, 77-78
  trademark registration in, 74
Forms
  attorneys creating, 171
  boilerplate language, 157
  contract forms, use of, 124
  review/update of, 177-178
Franchises, 170
Fraud
  as breach of contract defense, 116,
  120-121
  insurance claims, 158-159
FTC Act, 98-99, 100
FTC (Federal Trade Commission), 94-
97

G

General harassment issues, 31
Geographic area, competition in, 78
Glossary, 181-182
Goodwill
  geographic area, competition in, 78
  implementing non-disclosure
  policies, 79
  laws pertaining to, 62
  minimizing legal problems, 78-79
  non-competition agreements, 70-
  71, 78-79
  protection of, 70-71
  reasonable time period for non-
  competition, 78-79
  scope of restricted activity, 79

H

Handbooks for employees. *See*
Employee handbooks
Harassment. *See* Sexual harassment
Hazardous materials, businesses
involved in, 154
HIV status, protection of individuals
with, 45
Horizontal market allocation, 102
Horizontal price fixing, 101
Hostile work environment
harassment, 34-36

I

Identifying risks, 155
Implied warranty, 84
Impossibility of performance, 121
Impracticability of performance, 121

BOOKS

ENTREPRENEURING:
THE TEN COMMANDMENTS FOR BUILDING A GROWTH COMPANY
3RD EDITION

208 PAGES $14.95 (ITEM# AP-001)
ISBN 1-888925-02-7

This hard hitting book presents ten, proven operating principles for starting and building a successful company. With over 100,000 first-edition copies sold, noted entrepreneur and Stanford professor, Steven C. Brandt, offers practical guidance to entrepreneurs in the 90s.

- How to set objectives for yourself and the business
- How to select the right partners, investors, key employees
- How to define your product or service and market
- What to put in your business plan
- How to monitor and conserve cash and credit
- How to expand methodically
- How to avoid stress

This book covers startup issues essential for a solid foundation, including a guide to preparing an effective business plan. It gives details on crucial operating matters and points the way to entrepreneurial professionalism. Written to be used, it is a proven tool spiced with 26 real-life case studies and descriptive illustrations. The book is anchored in the fundamentals for business success.

"A primer for entrepreneurs. I wish I had read this book years ago; it would have saved me a lot of trouble!"

-Bob Hannah, Founder, R.S. Hannah Co.

If you want to build a business, here is your handbook.

To order this book, call **(800)360-6166**, or return the order form on the last page.

SPECIAL REPORTS

Get a quick management fix with our series of Special Reports. These concise, 10-20 page reports cover five specific areas of operating importance to any management team. They are designed to refresh your memory and stimulate your thinking.

❏ HOLDING ON TO GOOD PEOPLE: How To Cultivate (or Rebuild) Loyalty.

How do you hold on to a good team? Report shows how to use regular business activities, e.g., planning, to get people to bring their brains to work. Provides pointers on surveying (listening to) managers and employees to "take their pulse." Includes section on "How to Focus Your People in Tough Times".

(Item# SR01) $5.95

❏ EXECUTING PLANS: How To Get Your Key People To Pull Together In The Same Direction.

You've got a plan–now make it work! Covers how to boost implementation by determining the degree of plan buy-in that exists. Contains examples. Introduces organization design and culture as tools for getting desired things done. Includes a sample, 25-question Management Survey.

(Item# SR02) $5.95

❏ HIGH-IMPACT, OFFSITE MEETINGS: How To Get The Most Bang For Your Buck.

Are you really accomplishing anything at your gatherings? Describes how and why money is wasted, pitfalls to avoid, and how to plan and conduct major events to enhance behavior that supports the plans of your enterprise. Suggests how to walk what you talk!

(Item# SR03) $5.95

❏ BUSINESS PLANS THAT WORK: How To Develop A Plan You Will Actually Use.

Covers: Concept development, setting objectives, market analysis, production, marketing, organization & people, funds flow and financial projections, ownership considerations. Helps you prepare a blueprint for building your business. Includes a sample plan.

(Item# SR04) $5.95

❏ BASIC PROFIT MECHANICS: How To Make Money In Your Business.

Bottom line basics everyone *claims* to understand–but *do* they? Describes the "great profit myth." Explains fixed & variable costs, contribution margins, and break-even points in plain language. Includes major, practical ways to improve profitability. A classic!

(Item# SR05) $5.95

To order, call **1 (800) 360-6166**,
or return the order form on the last page.

How to order Books & Videos
from Archipelago Publishing

We hope you found *Stay Out Of Court and In Business* useful and helpful in building your business. If you have a business associate or relative who would benefit from having a copy of this book, here's how to order:

Single Copies
Please complete the ORDER FORM on the facing page and mail or fax it to us. To order by phone, **TOLL FREE**, call **1-800-360-6166**, 24 hours a day.

Quantity Orders
If you would like to distribute our books in your business or organization, or to your customers and clients as value-adding premiums, please call us immediately! Let us know how many copies you want, and we'll be happy to complete an order for you. We offer a substantial discount on orders of 25 or more books.

Archipelago Publishing
Build Your Business Guides
P.O. Box 1249
Friday Harbor, WA 98250
1-800-360-6166
Fax: 360-378-7097
email: info@buildyourbusiness.com

Build Your Business Guides
For more information about our *Build Your Business Guides* series, visit our website at **http://www.buildyourbusiness.com**. There you will find excerpts from our books & videos, links to selected business resources, and other materials to help you build your business.

Archipelago Publishing

ORDER FORM

To order copies of this book or other business-building materials, complete this form and send or FAX it to:

Archipelago Publishing
Build Your Business Guides
P.O. Box 1249
Friday Harbor, WA 98250
FAX# (360) 378-7097

ORDER BY PHONE TOLL FREE!
1-800-360-6166
Quantity Discounts Available

YES! Please send me the following items:

Qty	Title/Item#	Amount

TOTAL _____
(WA State Residents add 7.7% Sales Tax)_____
Shipping (see below)_____
TOTAL DUE:$_____

SHIP TO:
NAME:_____
ADDRESS:_____
CITY:_____ST:_____ ZIP:_____
DAYTIME PHONE:(   ) _____
(important)

Shipping Charges:
Priority Mail/First Class: $3.50 for up to two books. Call for larger orders.
Videos: $3.50 per video, or $15.00 for the series.

Payment:
Check Enclosed in the amount of $_____
Credit Card Orders: Visa or MasterCard Only

Card#_____ ex date:___/___

Signature:_____
Print Your Name:_____

For more information about any of our products & services, call
1-800-360-6166 or visit **http://www.buildyourbusiness.com**

Give your business a competitive edge!

Send now to receive a **FREE** poster of

THE TEN COMMANDMENTS
FOR
BUILDING A GROWTH COMPANY

"...the most valuable condensation of two years of business school I've ever read."

- Woody Howse, Cable & Howse Ventures

Please take a moment to complete and return the attached postage-paid card.
We'll rush you a FREE 8-1/2" x 11" poster copy of the *Ten Commandments for Building A Growth Company* by Steven C. Brandt.
These are the same secrets that thousands of business builders in Silicon Valley and around the globe have used to build successful companies. They have stood the test of time and are guaranteed to be an invaluable resource as you strive for success.

BUILD
YOUR
BUSINESS
GUIDES

For immediate information about our products and services call
1-800-360-6166 or visit **http://www.buildyourbusiness.com**